Design for Clerestory Window in Leaded glass without
Paint, by Arthur Louis Duthie.

DECORATIVE GLASS PROCESSES

Cutting, Etching, Staining and Other Traditional Techniques

ARTHUR LOUIS DUTHIE

WITH A NEW PREFACE BY
WILLIAM A. PRINDLE

The Corning Museum of Glass, Corning
IN ASSOCIATION WITH
DOVER PUBLICATIONS, INC., NEW YORK

Copyright © 1982 by The Corning Museum of Glass.
All rights reserved under Pan American and International
Copyright Conventions.

Published in Canada by General Publishing Company, Ltd.,
30 Lesmill Road, Don Mills, Toronto, Ontario.
Published in the United Kingdom by Constable and Company,
Ltd., 10 Orange Street, London WC2H 7EG.

This Dover edition, first published in 1982, is an unabridged
and unaltered republication of the work as originally published
by D. Van Nostrand Company, New York, in 1911 under the title
Decorative Glass Processes. A new Preface has been written
especially for the present edition by William A. Prindle.

Manufactured in the United States of America
Dover Publication, Inc.
180 Varick Street
New York, N.Y. 10014

Library of Congress Cataloging in Publication Data

Duthie, Arthur Louis.
    Decorative glass processes.
    Reprint. Originally published: New York : Van Nostrand Co.,
1911. (The Westminster series)
    Bibliography: p.
    1. Glass craft. I. Title. II. Series: Westminster series (New
York, N.Y.)
TT298.D87   1982   748.6   81-17302
ISBN 0-486-24270-6   AACR2

PREFACE TO
THE DOVER EDITION

Glassmaking, unfortunately, as is the case with many in-
dustries carried on through the years by artisans and their
apprentices, has long been cloaked in secrecy and portrayed
as a virtual "black art" to the uninitiated. Arthur Louis
Duthie's book on flat-glass techniques is a remarkable text;
its significance comes from both its informational content
and its historical context. His detailed cataloging made
Decorative Glass Processes the first comprehensive anthol-
ogy of flat-glass craftsmanship written in English up to
that time. The information it contains is formidable and
precise, and despite the extensive technology available today, few of the basic techniques have changed enough in
several hundred years to affect the usefulness of the material. Although some of the rather parochial illustrations
and antiquated terminology (notably the chemical references) may amuse some contemporary readers, the quality
and accuracy of the information demonstrate a sensitivity
to the material and are particularly refreshing in a field
not known for its exuberant, public sharing of technique.

Duthie's book is itself a "window" into turn-of-the-cen-
tury glass craftsmanship and, in fact, is practically a last
look at glassworking as it was practiced before the Indus-
trial Revolution changed the direction of the arts and the
role of craftsmen forever. These "modern" effects begin

to be noted in his intriguing section on patents and inclusion of the recent developments of sandblasting and electroplating as they pertain to glass. Even more important, though, are his references to the more general potential uses of glass architecturally and not solely as the usual ecclesiastical storyboards, the church windows.

Although the dynamics of the newly arrived twentieth century and the dramatic changes in all phases of life and art since the original publication of *Decorative Glass Processes* may seem to "date" the book, neither is its importance diminished nor is its information any less enlightening today.

WILLIAM A. PRINDLE

PREFACE TO
THE FIRST EDITION

THE present volume finds its reason for existence in the fact that no book has yet appeared dealing collectively with the various methods of glass decoration which it includes. We have many good books on Stained Glass; there are two or three works which touch lightly on Embossing, but nothing dealing with it in a thoroughly practical way, while nothing whatever seems to have appeared in print regarding Brilliant Cutting. One or two of the minor processes, such as Sand Blast, Crystalline, etc., also make what is practically a first appearance here.

The nomenclature employed is that of the workshop. To talk of "embossing" glass certainly seems absurd, but that is the accepted term, though its only excuse is that the acid produces a slight hollow on the surface of the glass. "Etching" is a much more satisfactory term in every respect, but "embossing" has become so sanctioned by use that it is useless to think of overthrowing it. So, too, with "brilliant cutting," which has no connection with diamonds, but is only a development of the glass engraving process which has so long been employed in the decoration of table and other hollow glassware.

The following pages are the result for the most part of the practical experience of the writer either as designer or executant, or both.   In one or two of the less important processes information which is not the result of practical experience has been obtained from reliable sources.

ARTHUR LOUIS DUTHIE

" CAMELOT,"
    ROUNDHAY, LEEDS,
      1908.

CONTENTS

LIST OF ILLUSTRATIONS

DECORATIVE GLASS PROCESSES

INTRODUCTION

Glass is a mixture of silicates, alkalies and earths, produced by fusing the ingredients. It is non-crystalline and structureless in its nature. Pure silica possesses in a high degree all the qualities which are required in glass, and glass can be made from it, but its great disadvantage is that it can only be worked at a temperature which is impossible under ordinary working conditions. Fine white sand, which is almost pure silica, is generally used in glass making and is rendered more fusible by the addition of other substances which have a lower melting point. The alkalies, potash and soda, which are used for this purpose, however, have the drawback of making the glass soluble in water and capable of being disintegrated by the action of the weather. To correct this alkaline earths are added— lime, baryta or magnesia—and so a glass is obtained which is both fusible and insoluble. The exact constitution of the glass and the proportions of ingredients, of course, vary widely under different circumstances. For instance, a black glass suitable for beer bottles has been made by simply melting a basaltic rock, or a mixture of basaltic rock with wood ashes ; sheet glass may be made of sand, limestone or chalk, sodium sulphate and broken glass; flint glass of sand, red lead, potassium carbonate and nitre.

Coloured glasses are produced by the addition of various metallic oxides to the " frit " before melting—red by the addition of copper or gold; yellow by silver, iron or antimony; blue by cobalt; green by copper; and so on--though it is stated that under certain conditions every colour in the spectrum can be produced by the use of iron alone, varying the temperature according to the colour required.

The ingredients are crushed, mixed well together and melted in a crucible. The molten " metal," as it is then called, is either cast or blown into shape, according to the character of the glass which is being made. In some cases, as when bottles or " slabs " are blown into a mould, there is something like a combination of the two.

Glass is proof against all acids except hydrofluoric, which is used for decorating it by means of etching. (A glass can be made from bones, however, which is proof against the action of fluoric.) It is capable of being ground or abraded by means of sand, emery, etc., and polished by putty powder and rouge. It is painted upon by means of pigments composed of highly fusible glass containing a large proportion of metallic oxide by way of colouring matter. This is fixed by firing in a kiln, when the pigment is melted and the surface of the glass sufficiently softened to admit of the colour sinking into it and becoming incorporated with it. It is cut into shapes of considerable variety by means of the diamond or the small steel wheel which is, under some circumstances, taking its place.

Owing to the power which glass has of refracting light and the fact that refraction takes place at the point of contact between the glass and the atmosphere—that is, the surface of the glass—the character of that surface is an all important factor in the appearance of the glass, apart from any consideration of colour or impurities in the material. Polished plate glass, having a perfectly smooth surface, which allows of the angles of refraction being alike for all rays of light which pass through it, is transparent, and under some circumstances practically invisible. Sheet glass ranks next to plate in this respect, its occasionally wavy surface producing distortion of objects seen through it. A certain amount of reflection is also possible when the rays of light which fall upon the surface of the glass are stronger than those which impinge upon the same point from behind, even in the case of perfectly clear glass without any backing. Both of these facts are turned to account in the manufacture of ornamental glasses, the surface being roughened either in casual haphazard fashion or in more or less mechanical pattern to produce a brilliant glittering effect, transparency being, of course, sacrificed. These glasses serve, in addition to the ornamental purpose primarily intended, a further useful purpose in scattering and diffusing the light which passes through them by means of the many differing angles of refraction given by the roughened surface, and so affording a means of improving the lighting of rooms which do not receive a sufficient amount of direct light.

The history of glass can be traced back to the very earliest periods of civilisation. Of its first discovery we have no authentic account, though more than one fantastic tale is told about it. The earliest accounts we have of it come from Egypt, where in a sculptured tomb found at Memphis there are representations of glass-blowing, along with other trades, such as carpentry, masonry, etc. The date of these sculptures must be somewhere about 3,900 B.C., and it is probable that glass was made by casting long before blowing was discovered; so we may safely put down the manufacture of glass as one of the oldest arts known to man. That there is no clue to the time and manner of its discovery is the more regrettable, as it seems hard to believe that such a discovery could have been altogether accidental in view of the high temperature required to fuse the silica.

In these early days the glass produced appears to have been all coloured and more or less opaque, anything approaching colourlessness and transparency not being attained until perhaps the times of the Greeks. The oldest examples of glass discovered in the tombs of Egypt and Assyria are in the form of beads, scarabs, amulets, etc., for personal decoration; while bottles, cups, vases, etc., came at a later date. Glass windows do not appear to have been used at all in Egypt—their first appearance is in Pompeii and Herculaneum. So we find that the history of glass in its ornamental is much older than in its useful capacity.

The ancient Egyptians attained a very remarkable degree of proficiency in glass work of various kinds—mosaic work, for instance, in which the pieces are fixed together by heating and with details so small as to require the aid of a magnifying glass to distinguish them. Engraving upon glass was also practised, and the manufacture of imitation gems was carried to great perfection. Glass bottles for holding wine and for other domestic purposes appear to have come into use about 2,000–1,500 B.C.

From Egypt glass was exported to all parts of the then known world, and when Egypt became in later and degenerate days a province of the Roman Empire, a large proportion of her tribute was paid in the form of glass ware.

The Phœnicians were, after the Egyptians, the most remarkable glass workers of ancient times, and their merchants and mariners carried their wares far and wide. Phœnician glass is frequently stamped with the maker's name and town in a manner which would lead one to believe that certain workers were looked upon as artists of surpassing genius, whose works had a value of their own.

Assyria also seems to have learned the art from Egypt, and many objects of glass have been discovered amongst the ruins of Nineveh and Babylon.

From Phœnicia the tradition passed on to Greece, but the Greeks appear to have preferred clay to glass, and did comparatively little with it. To them, however, we owe the magnificent Portland vase in the British Museum, which affords a most striking example of the wonderful perfection to which glass working had attained at this stage of its history. The body of the vase is of a dark blue glass overlaid, cameo fashion, with a coat of opaque white, which has been ground away upon a wheel leaving the white design in slight relief upon the blue. The Romans, on the other hand, in their day developed quite a craze for glass. The tribute of glass work paid by the Egyptians appeared merely to whet their appetite, and large quantities of glass of every kind were imported from Egypt. Then Egyptian workmen were brought to Rome in order the better to supply the demand by being on the spot, and from them by slow degrees the Romans learned the art and even in the long run outstripped their teachers. They used glass in a very great variety of ways—as bottles and drinking cups, for which they abandoned their old drinking cups of gold and silver, at their extravagant banquets—for personal ornaments—as pavements and wall decorations in the public baths and in their houses—even as drain pipes. The manufacture of imitation gems and cameos was largely carried on, and a story is told to the effect that the emperor Heliogabalus, wishing to play a practical joke upon some of his satellites, invited them to a great feast, at which, in place of the usual extravagant delicacies, the table was covered with imitations in glass or pottery of meats and fruits of the most rare and beautiful kinds.

Window glass, as has already been noted, was probably first used by the Romans, who also made use of it for forcing frames for horticulture. In Pompeii the windows of the public baths were filled in with plate glass slightly obscured on one side to prevent people on the outside from seeing in—one of these plates, a single pane of cast glass, measuring 3 ft. 8 in. by 2 ft. 8 in. Up to this time and for some time afterwards, windows were generally filled in with mica, alabaster, linen, etc. This window glass was greenish in colour and far from being perfectly transparent, though there is some reason for believing that transparent glass had been made in Greece as early as 360 B.C. Pausias, of Sicyon, at that time painted a picture of " Drunkenness," in which the face of a female figure showed clearly through the transparent glass of the drinking cup which she was raising to her lips. The Romans also occasionally set pieces of glass in frames of copper and lead, much in the same way as in leaded lights of a later date. As the old glass workers seem to have had greater difficulty in producing white glass than coloured, one would naturally expect to find coloured glass used in windows at an early date, especially as so much of it was used in wall and floor decoration. As a matter of fact, however, all efforts seem to have been directed at first towards obtaining colourless glass in windows. The first mention of the use of coloured glass in windows places it about 337 A.D. in the church of St. Paul's, near Rome, built by Constantine. "In the windows are displayed glass of varied colours, as brilliant as the fields of flowers in spring." These must, of course, have been mosaic windows, either in metal frames or in pierced stone slabs. Horace writes of pictures painted on glass with which he adorned his room, but there is no reason for supposing that these were painted with vitreous pigments and fixed by firing. Painted glass windows appear to date from about the time of Charlemagne, 800 A.D. The oldest painted glass now in existence is that in the windows of the Abbey of St. Denis, placed there when the church was rebuilt in 1140, while the oldest in England is probably that in the choir windows of Canterbury Cathedral, rebuilt in 1174.

In Cairo at the present day are to be seen numbers of windows in which small pieces of coloured glass are let into a framework of plaster. This system seems to have been in use in the East for some centuries. A number of windows in the Mosque of Omar, which was erected in 1528, on the site of the Temple of Jerusalem, were executed in this way. The plaster is strengthened by ribs of iron and rods of cane embedded in the wider portions of the framework. In work of this sort the glass and plaster—light and darkness—are practically equal in superficial area. It is a direct development of the earliest Roman practice in which small pieces of glass were set into pierced openings in large slabs of stone.

The credit of the invention of glass mirrors is probably due to the Egyptians, possibly to the Phœnicians. Aristotle says " that if metal or pebbles have to be polished to serve as mirrors, glass or crystal require to be lined with a leaf of metal to throw back the image presented to them," which seems to indicate that metal-backed glass mirrors were not uncommon articles in his time. The glass must, however, have been of poor quality as regards smoothness and transparency, so it is not surprising that the use of metallic mirrors was still continued. Amongst other devices was one in which blown glass was covered inside with lead while still hot. In 1317 the Venetians succeeded in making mirrors by coating plates of glass with an amalgam of tin and mercury—a process which continued in vogue until it was ousted during last century by the chemical deposition of silver now in use.

So it appears that three at least of the processes with which we are concerned date from pre-Christian times—Mosaic, leading and engraving or cutting. Painting dates from the eighth century of the Christian era. The use of hydrofluoric acid was introduced towards the close of the eighteenth or in the beginning of the nineteenth century, while the first use of the sand blast is so recent as 1870.

Our word " glass " appears to have originated in the

ancient British word "glas," the name of the bluish-
green pigment with which the Britons painted their bodies
and which was called by Pliny *glastrums*, by Cæsar
vitrum. Strabo records that the Britons made glass vessels
of a bluish-green colour prior to the Roman invasion.
It is probable that they had learned the art from the
Phœnicians who visited this country in search of tin and
other merchandise. Fragments of glass, both window
glass and other, have been found in ruins of Roman buildings
in England, showing that it was in fairly common use at
that period. With the fall of the Roman power, however,
it would appear that the making of glass was discontinued,
and the art forgotten, since in the seventh century Benedict,
Bishop of Wearmouth, had to send to France for workmen to glaze the windows of the church which he was
building. About the same period St. Wilfred introduced
glass into the windows of St. Peter's Church, York, and
probably in response to a demand for glass caused by these
and other restorations and buildings an attempt was made
to establish a window glass manufactory at Newcastle-upon-
Tyne, but without success. In Ireland some remarkable
specimens of early mosaic work are to be seen in the Lismore
crosier, originally made for a Bishop of Lismore who died
in 1112, and in the cross of Cong. Some glass cups are
preserved in the museum of the Irish Academy which are
supposed to date from the ninth and tenth centuries. In
Scotland very few traces of ancient glass have been found,
but curious contributions to the history of glass are to be
found in the "vitrified forts" which are to be found in
several places in the north. Whether the vitrifaction be
the result of accident or design it is impossible to say, but

the fact remains that walls of undressed stone which have been erected for purposes of fortification have been vitrified, so thoroughly in some cases that stones have been melted down. This may have been the result of burning watch fires upon the walls, but the fires must have been of exceptional size and heat to produce such results in open air. Throughout the Middle Ages England followed, more or less, the lead of Continental workers in window and other glass, at times holding her own very well, but never apparently leading the way. At the present day keen commercial competition has left the window glass supply of this country almost entirely in the hands of Belgium, both as to sheet glass and plate; but for the more expensive coloured glass required for stained glass and other decorative work, English makers can quite easily lead the way.

The advantages which glass presents from a decorative point of view are permanency, cleanliness, brilliance and colour. The only other materials which offer the same qualities in anything like comparative degree are faience and tiles which, with their brilliant glazes, are practically glass backed with clay. Opportunities for the use of glass in the shape of mosaic, etc., for mural decoration are not so frequently made use of at the present time as they might be, a great deal of material and work being used which is purely of a temporary character requiring frequent renewal. The fuller, richer and more delicate colouring which glass offers in comparison with paint, wood, marble and other materials will, it is hoped, meet with wider recognition as a knowledge of colour-harmony and a love for really beautiful rather than showy things spreads abroad. There are, of course, many opportunities for improvement in the processes at present in vogue. Especially in the way of enamelling in both transparent and opaque colours upon large sheets of transparent and opaque glass there appears to me to be a considerable field for artistic and useful work. The difficulties in the way are considerable—whether they can be overcome or not it is impossible at present to say, but it is more than probable that overcoming them is merely a question of time and study—of thought and experiment.

Fig. 1.—Design for Chapel Glazing,
by Walter J. Pearce.

CHAPTER I

KINDS OF GLASS

PRACTICALLY every kind of glass which has ever been made can be turned to account in some decorative process, whether it be the simplest and cheapest sheet glass or the most beautiful " antique "—we have seen broken bottles used with good effect in leaded figure work. The number of ornamental glasses grows from day to day, so much so as to show at the present a very formidable number. Many of them naturally are somewhat limited in their sphere of usefulness for various reasons, having been introduced in some cases in response to a demand for novelty and artistic effect. The latter demand is rather poorly met on the whole, though there are varying opinions on the point, and many people are perfectly satisfied with what to others is little short of an abomination. The majority are naturally intended to be seen by transmitted light, but a number of them, opalescent or iridescent in character, are also useful when placed so as to reflect light, and advantage is taken of this fact to turn them to a number of purposes which they were not at first calculated to fulfil. Considerable ingenuity has been displayed in one or two instances in taking advantage of and enhancing these qualities, and very successful results have been attained.

A description of the glasses in most general use in the processes which we propose to study, with notes of the manner in which they are most successfully used, will be necessary here, along with an approximate price list to show their relative value. Artistic value and commercial value do not in all cases correspond, as is perhaps to be expected, but with a few exceptions they may be said to do so. Design is, of course, the supreme factor in this respect, a good design in cheap glasses appearing more valuable than a poor design in which more valuable and much more beautiful glasses can only look tawdry. Generally speaking, a small quantity of the more valuable glasses goes a long way, and judicious treatment in this respect often admits of their use when economic considerations would otherwise forbid. The different processes by which they are manufactured are of great interest as accounting in most cases for their peculiar characteristics and showing how these are produced, but it will not help us in any way to do more than mention them in passing.

The simplest and cheapest is, of course, *Sheet* glass, which in spite of its simplicity, or perhaps because of it, has a wide range of usefulness. It is made by blowing in cylinders 5 feet or more in length, which are afterwards split open and flattened out in a kiln. The majority of it comes from the Continent, principally Belgium. Its different thicknesses are distinguished as 15 oz., 21 oz., 26 oz., 32 oz., etc., these figures representing the approximate weight per superficial foot. It is divided by selection into first, second, third, and fourth qualities according to its freedom from waves, air-bubbles, and other defects. It is largely used for leaded lights, where transparency is required at a low price, and also for the cheapest class of embossed and brilliant cut work. *Obscured Sheet* glass is also used for embossing and brilliant cutting. It was at one time produced by means of hand grinding, but is now done entirely by means of the sand-blast. Sheet glass is also *Enamelled* in various stencilled patterns with white enamel. and stained with silver stain, but, owing to the hardness of the metal, a very strong stain is required. This Enamelled Sheet had a considerable vogue at one time for screen work in private houses and elsewhere, but has now been superseded, except for repairs, by embossed work or leaded lights.

Patent Plate is made by grinding and polishing selected sheet glass on both sides, so removing the wavy surface which would otherwise have the effect of distorting images seen through it and producing what is practically thin plate glass. For a good class of leaded lights for living rooms it is much superior to sheet glass as eliminating distortion and is frequently used on that account. There are, however, people who ask for sheet glass because of the quaint effect produced by the distortion, and who even welcome the use of the now almost obsolete *Crown* glass in order that the distortion may be more marked. *Crown* glass is made in flat discs of about 4 feet diameter by a " spinning " process, the metal being changed from a bulb shape to the disc by the action of centrifugal force. The result of this spinning is that all the waves on the surface are curvilinear and concentric, while the centre of the disc where the " pontil " is broken off shows a big bull's-eye knob, which used to be regarded as waste, but is now sought after for leaded light work.

Rough Cast Plate is produced by rolling and can be had in thicknesses of $\frac{1}{4}$ inch, $\frac{3}{8}$ inch, $\frac{1}{2}$ inch, and upwards. It is frequently used for skylights, painted and stained in various styles, and can be bent to practically any curve to fit the spherical surfaces of domes, etc. It answers very well for painting and staining, the metal being softer than sheet glass, and some very good and varied effects can be produced with it. It is non-transparent and therefore recommends itself for use in ceiling lights, etc., where there is an external glass roof the frame of which would show badly through a clearer glass. There is practically no limit to size. It can be embossed with white acid and has been tried for brilliant cutting, but here its wavy surface renders it quite useless, destroying the outline of the design, which is of course dependent upon a regular level surface.

Patent Rolled Plate is also non-transparent, and one side shows a series of corrugated ridges about $\frac{1}{16}$ inch apart. These give it a mechanical look which makes it less useful for decoration, but it can be had with stained spot diapers upon it, which make it more attractive. Indeed this is the only form in which it may be said to enter the field of decorative glasses at all. It is useless for leading, embossing, or brilliant cutting. It is one of the least transparent of all colourless glasses, but it transmits a wonderful amount of light, which it diffuses very well, and so is useful from a utilitarian point of view for screens and borrowed lights.

Polished Plate glass is made from rough cast by grinding and polishing with emery and rouge. Its principal use from our point of view is in embossing and brilliant cutting. In size it is, of course, similar to rough cast, and can be had in sheets as large as 12 feet by 10 feet, or even larger when specially required, as, for instance, in shop windows—the record size at present is somewhere about 20 feet by 14 feet. In thickness it ranges from $\frac{3}{16}$, $\frac{1}{4}$, $\frac{5}{16}$, $\frac{3}{8}$ inch upwards. It lends itself readily to staining, being the same metal as the rough cast which we have already noted, and staining is occasionally used to enhance the effect of embossed and brilliant cut work. For leaded lights it is occasionally cut into more or less elaborate forms and its edges bevelled, when it gives a very brilliant though rather hard effect. Plates of almost any size can be embossed, though the difficulty and risk are naturally very great in the case of a large plate. In brilliant cut work the limit of size is about 4 feet square for average work—beyond that size only very simple designs, such as straight lines, spots, etc., which can be done without swinging the plate round, are possible.

The remaining glasses which we have to consider are mainly—some of them entirely—used for leaded and painted work. Of these the commonest is *Rolled Cathedral*, which is produced in sheets from 5 feet to 7 feet long and 28 inches wide. This is made in white, in tints, and in a variety of more or less pronounced colours, a large proportion of which cannot, from an artistic point of view, be commended. It is non-transparent and can be used wherever a moderate amount of obscurity is required for screens, etc. For painting and staining the white and tinted varieties are most useful. The white stains very well, as also do the greenish tints, but the yellowish tints are not so susceptible to the action of the silver. For cheap leaded light work it is extremely useful on account of its variety of tints and the ease with which it can be cut, while its uniform thickness makes it very easily handled in leading.

Double rolled cathedral is a later introduction. It is more brilliant, the wavy surface being rather more open, and a little more transparent than single rolled. It is made in white and tints, and for painting and leading can be used in the same way as the single variety.

Muffled is practically a sheet glass, being blown in cylinders in a similar fashion. It is distinguished by a peculiar rippling surface which is rather more marked on one side than the other, and which frequently varies considerably in the length of a single sheet. This surface is produced at an early stage in the process of making, by blowing the bubble of glass into a mould, the interior of which is marked with the desired pattern in what might be called a compressed form. When the glass is removed from the mould and stretched to the full-sized cylinder, the pattern becomes distended and loses some of its regularity, the upper part of the cylinder naturally, through the weight of the lower part, having the pattern more smoothed out. It is very translucent and diffuses light well, while, in its rougher varieties at least, it makes a rather more effective screen than Rolled. Its range of colour is similar to Rolled, and it is equally useful for painting, staining, and leading. Its greater brilliance renders it more popular than Rolled for the cheaper class of leaded lights, but in artistic value it is rather inferior.

Rippled is a rolled glass with a very strong surface marking somewhat like muffled, but too pronounced and rather too regular to be altogether pleasant. It may be looked upon as a sort of imitation of muffled.

Figured Rolled is produced by means of a machine having rollers with engraved surfaces which impress their pattern upon the surface of the glass. The artistic value of these patterns is practically *nil*. The glass is used principally in large sheets for screens where diffusion of light without transparency is required, and though it occasionally finds its way into the cheaper class of leaded lights, the effect is almost invariably as bad as it can be. In large sheets, on the other hand, the effect of the patterns, which vary considerably in size, is brilliant and, on account of their power of diffusing light, frequently very useful. White and some dozen light tints are to be had.

Flemish is another variety of rolled glass somewhat similar in character to Double Rolled, but having a much larger "wave," and very much heavier in body. It is made in white and tints, and its peculiar character of surface makes it extremely useful in leaded lights where a brilliant effect is required in a window much overshadowed by other buildings, muffled glass being also advantageous in such a position. Against a clear sky it loses almost all its effect and becomes no better than ordinary rolled. It should be noted that all the glasses with roughened or wavy surfaces come into this category and do not show to advantage unless viewed against a comparatively dark background with the light falling upon them at a more or less acute angle.

Crapene is a recent introduction very similar to Flemish, but more mechanical in its marking and therefore not quite so good in effect.

Variegated and Opalescent Rolled glasses are valuable on account of the very great variety of broken colour which

they afford, and which at times places them, for certain
purposes at least, almost on a level with the most expensive
Antiques. Variegated Rolled was first made in England
some twenty years ago, but did not "catch on." Since
then it has been revived and Opalescent Rolled introduced
by American enterprise, and both have been extensively
used in the recent "boom" of leaded light work. They
are both made with "rippled" as well as "rolled" surfaces,
the "rippled" having a peculiar glitter which is very useful
under certain conditions and in small pieces. These glasses,
as a class, are very bad for cutting, as they are badly
annealed. The pressure of the diamond is quite sufficient
to smash a large sheet, and the unequal and sometimes
"thready" surface is apt to make the cut a very unsteady
one. They cut very well under the wheel, however, and it
is generally found best to use it alone on glass of this
nature. The opalescent has rather a bad fault in that the
milkiness produced by the tin oxide which enters largely
into the colouring matter of the glass is glaringly visible
from the outside, but this defect can be turned into an
advantage where ornament, and especially lettering, is
required to show to the outside, as in the case of signboards, door panels, etc. Moreover, it will not stand firing,
the milkiness becoming much more turbid and dense during
the process. Variegated glasses change colour in the kiln,
generally becoming much darker. There is also a very
great risk of breakage, both with opalescent and variegated,
the imperfect annealing making them specially subject to
"fire cracks." When it is necessary or desirable to use
these glasses for painted work it is usual to "plate" them
with clear sheet, the painting being done upon the sheet

glass. Their chief value, however, is for leaded light work, where their beautiful broken colour lends itself specially to combination with light backgrounds and varying thicknesses of lead.

One of the most beautiful of the opalescent glasses is *Opalescent Reamy Sheet.* The opal is flashed upon one side in irregular streaks and splashes and is nowhere solid white. It is only made in white. Being a flashed glass it is open to treatment with acid. It has been used with great success for lettering on doors for restaurants, etc., by aciding away the background and leaving the letters white. The result is particularly happy in producing a letter which is varied in quality and perfectly legible without showing the staring, chalky effect generally inseparable from opal glass. A very rich effect can also be produced by embossing clear ornament upon an opal ground. This glass is worthy of being better known and more widely used, as its capabilities are by no means exhausted by the uses suggested above.

Under the heading of *Antiques* we find a great variety of most useful glasses—*Pot, Flashed, Streaky,* and *Venetian.* *Pot metal* glass is that in which the colouring material is mixed thoroughly with the other ingredients during the process of melting—the glass is coloured right through, and the only variation which can be obtained is a slight shading from light to dark owing to the varying thickness of the glass, which may range from $\frac{1}{16}$ inch to $\frac{1}{4}$ inch within a square foot. *Flashed* glass, on the other hand, is not coloured right through, but has merely a very thin film of colour laid upon one side of a sheet of white, pale green, yellow, or pale blue. The practice probably arose from the great power of the colouring materials used to produce ruby

—-pot metal ruby (!) would be positively black—but it has developed other advantages, as, for instance, the possibility of removing or modifying the " flash " by means of hydro-fluoric acid, and also of modifying the colour by flashing it upon differently-coloured bases. Ruby is the colour most frequently produced in this way, but blue is also to be had, and occasionally green. At one time the number of colours made in flashed glass was much greater than it is now. Purples and yellows were to be had, but of course the value of the latter was largely diminished by the fact that a very similar effect could be more conveniently produced on white glass by means of stain. *Streaky* glasses are made by dipping the blowpipe successively into pots of differently coloured " metal" and working the small quantities thus collected into one mass, the different colours remaining more or less distinct in hue, but being distributed in streaks across the surface. Greens, whites, and yellows are the colours most frequently treated in this way and are extremely useful for high-class work. Streaky antique has the disadvantage which has already been mentioned in connection with variegated rolled—it is very apt to change colour in the kiln and even to break, though in this latter respect it is much safer than variegated rolled. It is also apt to show a number of minute cracks known as " crissles," any of which may, during cutting or afterwards, develop into a break. *Venetian* glass is made by blowing a " bubble " of glass into a cylindrical iron mould having a strongly-marked screw pattern on its interior surface. It is then removed to another mould with a reversed, or left-handed, screw pattern. Between the two is produced a lozenge pattern which loses some of its definition and regularity in the subsequent stretching of the bubble to a full-sized "muff." It is a very brilliant glass, but on account of the strongly-marked pattern it is not very suitable for use in large pieces. Cut up into small pieces its brilliant lozenges make admirable "jewels" for ornamental leaded lights. The range of colour is confined to light tints and opalescents.

Antique glasses are all made by blowing in cylinders or "muffs" which are afterwards split and flattened out in a kiln into sheets of about 24 inches by 16 inches. The range of colour is practically unlimited. "Whites" include pure whites, "warm" whites, "streaky" whites, and "dark" whites, which might be called light greens. Ruby is flashed upon white, warm white, green white, yellow, and blue. Blue is flashed upon pure white and greenish white. Pot metal colours range through yellows, greens, blues, purples, browns, pinks, etc., and from light to dark, in a bewildering variety. Sometimes thick edges of sheets become so dark as to transmit no light at all. Antique glasses, except perhaps streaky, which is sometimes troublesome if not well annealed, cut well under either diamond or wheel, and stand firing well, except that some of the softer metals, greens particularly, come rather near melting point and are apt to lose their brilliance and sparkle. Neutral colours, too, are sometimes apt to change colour, becoming darker. Antique whites take silver stain very readily, but those which are greenish in hue are rather apt to show the stain on the outside as an opaque-looking yellow smudge. Antique glass is the main stock-in-trade of the painter of memorial windows, to whom its range and richness of colour and the ease with which it can be cut, painted, and fired are invaluable. One frequently hears complaints that the art of glass-making has been lost, and that no modern glass can compare with the glass of the old windows, but, as a matter of fact, the case stands entirely the other way. A hundred years ago such statements were doubtless true enough, but the state of affairs has entirely changed since then, and the modern glass painter has a variety of glass and a quality of glass that might well make the old monks and their co-workers turn in their graves with envy. There is certainly some fine glass in the thirteenth and fourteenth century windows at Canterbury, York, and elsewhere, but there is none that cannot be equalled and surpassed by the modern glass-maker. Apart from the mellowing effects of time, the richness of a great deal of old glass is entirely dependent on the fearless way in which strong colours such as ruby, blue, and green are thrown together, generally in small pieces, and wherever that system is adopted in modern work the effect is at least as good.

Perhaps the finest colours in Antique glass are those obtained by flashing Gold Pink upon white, yellow, blue, and purple. The colouring matter in this case is actually gold, which supplies an economic reason for flashing the glass instead of making pot metal, and the pink produced upon white glass is of a very beautiful quality. Flashing it upon a yellow base brings it to something like a scarlet, upon blue produces a fine violet, and upon purple a rich colour unapproachable by any other means. Gold Pink is also made in opalescent and streaky forms, which are generally more useful for jewel-like bits in good leaded lights than for memorial window work. Somewhat similar to Antique in richness and quality of colour—the metal is the same—but possessing a peculiar quality of its own to which words would do scant justice, are *Norman Slab* or *Bottle* glass and *Wood White* bottle glass. These are produced by blowing a bubble of glass into an iron box-shaped mould. Where the soft metal first touches the mould it will be perhaps half an inch thick, but as it gradually expands into the corners it quickly thins away and occasionally bursts in the extreme angles. When turned out of the mould it looks like a glorified pickle bottle or Leclanché electric cell—split up the corners, it produces four slabs of glass about 7 inches by 5 inches, and one 5 inches by 5 inches. These show a fairly dark spot of colour in the centre where the metal is thickest, growing lighter towards the edges as it grows thinner. There is a peculiar *watery* quality about this glass which cannot be found in any other and is specially valuable in leaded light work for domestic purposes. For ecclesiastical work the brilliant depth and translucent jewel-like quality of the colour add very great richness to any colour scheme. Streaky opalescent and gold pink are all to be had in this form, while the range of colour is practically equal to that of antique. *Wood White* is a very pure silvery white glass made in the same way, of about the same size and also smaller—about 5 inches by $3\frac{1}{2}$ inches—and is frequently used in its original size for plain square leaded lights where a quaint, colourless effect is required.

Of a similar nature to the above are Pressed Slabs. They are made from the same metal as Antique and Norman, but shaped into pieces about 8 inches by 8 inches, and smaller, by stamping. It is very similar in quality to Norman, and

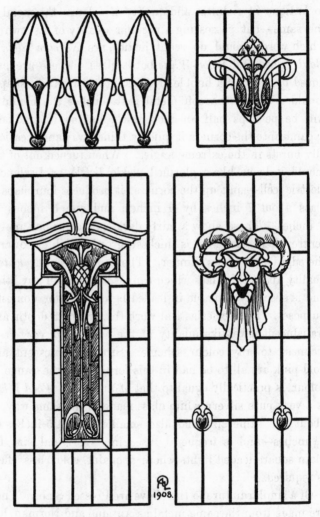

Fig. 2.—Designs for Leaded Lights, by A. L. Duthie.

is produced in a large variety of colours, including many fine streaky and variegated effects.

Amongst other "fancy" glasses of a similar nature may be mentioned "*Luna*" glass. This is a muff glass, similar to Antique, with a peculiar iridescent surface. Over the body of the metal are laid a number of streaks which look as they might have been produced by a very soft enamel poured on in little streams which cross and recross in every direction. Owing to its iridescence it would be most useful in domestic and furniture work.

Anbitty is a very fine glass of a "sheet" nature varying from an almost transparent surface to a surface as obscure as muffled. It is made in light tints, some of which become strong enough to be called greens. The lighter tints stain very well, and the peculiar quality of surface is eminently suitable for high-class painted and stained work of Renaissance or semi-natural design. Anbitty is produced by keeping the molten metal at a certain temperature for some hours before blowing. Under these conditions the glass tends to crystallise, and the peculiar texture is due to the presence of numerous minute crystals in the body of the sheet.

Fluted sheet, though hopelessly crude and mechanical in large surfaces, is very useful in small pieces and narrow "lines" in leaded lights.

Tinted or *Cathedral sheet* is not so much used now as it was some years ago, having been ousted by the cheaper *rolled*. It has rather a quaint effect, because though tinted it is still almost as transparent as clear sheet. It is useful for church and chapel windows as well as for domestic work.

The *bull's-eyes* which formed the centres of sheets of

crown glass have had such a vogue for leaded lights that they have even been taken out of old windows in cottages, farmhouses, workshops, and stables to supply the demand for them. They are now specially manufactured for leaded light work. Somewhat resembling them, but circular in form and having a very much smaller and thinner "eye," are *roundels*, which have always been largely used in leaded lights and are characteristic of German and Italian windows. They are made in an infinite variety of colour and size, but require to be very carefully handled with regard to design to prevent their looking commonplace. White roundels painted with suitable patterns and stained gain considerably in interest. In addition to roundels there are also to be had a great variety of *stamped pateræ* and facetted *jewels*, the majority of which cannot be recommended for use in good-class work, though the plainer of them can frequently be turned to very good account by a smart designer. Some further remarks on the use of the foregoing glasses will be found under the heading of Design in Chapter II.

Opal glass, useful for lettering, advertising devices, etc., on account of its opaque white surface, is made both as pot metal and flashed, the latter being, of course, capable of being treated with acid, giving white lettering or ornament on a clear ground, or *vice versâ*. It is also possible to obtain pot opal glass flashed with turquoise, yellow, orange, and ruby, which can be treated with acid, removing the coloured veneer and exposing the white base as may be required.

Herewith is given an approximate price list of the various glasses mentioned above, which is intended to give an idea of the *relative* value as a guide to the freedom with which they can be used as regards economy. Some of them vary slightly from time to time owing to market fluctuations, but the following will be sufficiently accurate as a guide to *relative* value.

COMPARATIVE LIST OF GLASS PRICES.

SUBJECT TO MARKET FLUCTUATIONS.

	Per sq. ft. s. d.		Per sq. ft. s. d.
Sheet glass—		Antique streaky . .	2 0
15 oz. . . .	0 2½	Venetian white . . .	1 9
21 oz. . . .	0 3½	,, pot metal . .	2 0
26 oz. . . .	0 4½	,, streaky . .	3 6
Patent plate . . .	1 6	,, opalescent . .	3 6
Crown	1 3	Norman slabs (according to	
Rough cast plate . .	0 4	size) 2s. 6d. to 21s. per	
Patent rolled plate . .	0 4	doz.	
Polished plate . . .	1 6	Wood white (according to	
Rolled Cathedral . .	0 4	size) 2s. 6d. to 15s. per	
Double rolled Cathedral .	0 5	doz.	
Muffled	0 6	Pressed slabs, from 12s. per	
Rippled . .; . .	0 6	doz. upwards.	
Figured rolled . . .	0 6		
Flemish	0 8	Luna	2 6
Crapene	0 8	Anbitty . . .	0 8
Variegated and Opal-		Fluted sheet . . .	0 4
escent rolled . . .	1 6	Cathedral sheet . . .	0 6
Opalescent reamy . .	1 6	Bull's - eyes (according to	
Antique whites . .	1 6	size) 4s. to 48s. per doz.	
,, pot metals .	1 4	Opal—	
,, rubys .	2 6	Pot metal . . .	0 6
,, gold pink .	4 0	Flashed . . .	1 6

CHAPTER II

THE practice of joining together small pieces of glass by means of bands of lead probably had its origin in the Middle Ages in the fact that it was only possible then to make glass in small pieces which would have to be joined together to make up the size necessary for the glazing of windows. The opportunity thus given for the introduction of differently coloured glasses was, of course, quickly recognised and paved the way for the development of stained glass windows, but at the same time for both ecclesiastical and domestic work the use of leaded patterns in clear and light tinted glass continued, and many fine geometrical patterns of mediæval origin are to be found both in this country and abroad. The interest added to a window by a leaded pattern is unquestionable. The use of lead work lapsed almost entirely during the Renaissance period, but since then it has revived and at the present time is being used in buildings of all styles. The process in itself, however, is still the same as was employed by the mediæval craftsman. The diamond and the wheel have replaced the red-hot iron for cutting, and hydraulic-drawn lead has ousted cast lead, but otherwise the work goes on as before. It is essentially a handicraft. The first step is the making of a full-sized drawing showing the size of each piece of glass, the lines upon it representing the heart of the lead.

From this drawing the glass is cut to the required shapes. The glass is then built up into the lead frame, the drawing again serving as a guide. The completed panel then has to be cemented to make it thoroughly weatherproof, after which, except in the smallest sizes, the copper wire ties which are to secure it to the iron saddle-bars are soldered on, and, a reasonable time having been allowed for the cement to harden, the panel is ready for fixing.

The tools required for leaded light work are of a very simple character. For the cutting of the glass the diamond is widely used, but not universally so, as it has been found in practice that the American wheel glass cutter is equally useful on most glasses, and on some of rough or undulating surface even superior. The diamond, to cut properly, must be always at a particular angle with the surface—an angle which varies with every diamond and which must be affected by an undulating surface: to the wheel all angles are alike, and the angle at which the handle of it is held is a matter of the convenience of the workman. Most men hold it practically vertical. The diamond in traversing a rough or "reamy" surface runs a risk of being torn from its setting which the wheel is free from. For cutting round the edges of paper patterns or moulds, the diamond is not quite so likely to run over the edge of the paper as the wheel, but in a practised hand the wheel can be made to follow the edge with wonderful precision. For cutting large sheets of glass the diamond is safest, as requiring less weight upon it and so minimising risk of breakage, but with glasses such as Venetian Lozenge, Opalescent Rolled, Flemish, etc., especially with intricate shapes, the wheel does much better work. The wheel, however, labours under the great disadvantage that all, or nearly all, those which reach this side of the Atlantic have handles so very badly shaped as to render the holding of them and working with them a really painful matter.   The handle is short and badly shaped, and can only be made usable in most cases by wrapping it up in rag bandages or enclosing it in a piece of rubber gas tube.   In addition to this the "block" is absurdly light and utterly useless for tapping with, its weight being still further reduced by two or three notches, which are apparently intended as grozing irons, but are generally utterly useless for such a purpose.   Occasionally one comes across a wheel with the wooden handle resembling a diamond, but even then the grozing notches are present. What is wanted is a wheel set in a block of the same size and weight as that used for diamonds, with a wooden handle of correct shape, and some day, I hope, we may be able to get it, if we only keep on asking.

For cutting a number of circular pieces the "circle board" is very useful, ensuring accuracy and also working with much greater speed than hand cutting.   The cutting point in this case is, of course, a diamond, but owing to the steadiness with which the machine holds it, it works with good results on some kinds of glass on which the hand diamond does not give good results.   For pieces of less than 3 inches diameter, however, hand cutting with a paper pattern is generally best.   Two or three pairs of wire-pliers with varying widths of jaws will be required for "grozing," one at least of which should have cutters for cutting wire ties.

Straight-edges, set-squares, and T-squares of various sizes will also be required.

For the lead work are required—a lead knife, bent knife (or stopping knife), pliers, lathykin, soldering bolt, bench nails, etc. The lead knife is generally made from a palette knife, the blade being broken off chisel fashion and ground to a sharp edge. The handle is then weighted with lead, or, preferably, block tin as being harder, and becomes a useful hammer for driving bench nails and "knocking up" pieces of glass into their proper positions. To accomplish this weighting it is usual to cut grooves in the wood of the handle as illustrated in Fig. 3. Then the handle is wrapped around with several thick-nesses of brown paper to form a mould. The edge of the knife is then stuck into a wooden bench to hold it upright, the tin melted in a ladle and poured into the mould.

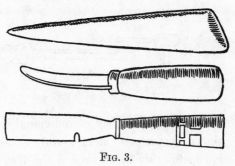

FIG. 3.

As soon as it has set, the paper is removed and the tin smoothed down with a file, if necessary, and finished off by scraping with a broken edge of glass. A notch filed in the edge of the blade, as indicated in the sketch, will be found useful for drawing nails and so saving the continual exchange of lead knife for pliers in leading up. The stopping knife is not really a knife at all, but rather a sort of handle or hook which may be inserted under the flange of the lead to raise the work slightly from the bench, and which is also used for opening up the flanges when "stopping in." A very good one can

D.G.P.

be made by bending the blade of an oyster opener by heating it in the fire and retempering it. The handle of it may also be loaded, but this is not so useful on the bent knife as on the lead knife. Pliers are required for grozing, stretching lead, pulling nails, etc. The latrican, larrikin, or lathykin—its name varies strangely, and Mr. Whall's version, lathykin (a little lath), seems the most likely to be correct—is a piece of hard close-grained wood, such as lancewood, or of bone, about 7 inches long, $1\frac{1}{4}$ inches wide at the butt, and $\frac{1}{4}$ inch at its thickest part. The shape

FIG. 4.

varies with the fancy of individual workers, but the one shown is perhaps most useful. The point of it is used for opening up the flanges of the lead before inserting the glass, while the broad, flat butt end is used for closing them down again afterwards. Bench nails are required for holding glass and lead in position during the process of leading—the most useful form is the $1\frac{1}{4}$ inch lasting nail used by shoemakers.

Soldering bolts heated by gas are almost universally used now in preference to those heated in a fire. They can be obtained from any manufacturer of gas apparatus, notably from Messrs. Fletcher, Russell & Co., of Warrington, who make one of a very light and effective pattern. A bolt in which the copper bit takes the form of a length of copper rod about $\frac{5}{16}$ inch diameter held by an adjusting screw is most serviceable, as it allows of the copper being moved downwards as it wears away under the continual heating and filing. (Fig. 4.)

Bench laths of white wood, about 2 inches wide by $\frac{3}{8}$ inch thick, are used to hold lights in shape and position while on the bench. Pencils of French chalk will be found

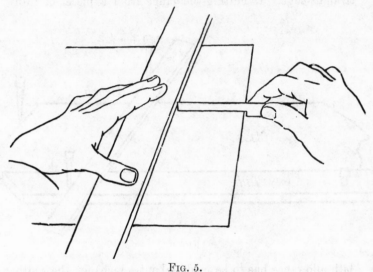

Fig. 5.

useful for marking the surface of the glass as a guide for cutting and grozing.

Many devices of various kinds are used to facilitate and expedite the cutting of the glass for lead light work. In the cutting of squares, where it is absolutely necessary to ensure accuracy of size and angles, gauges are required. The simplest of these is the hand gauge shown in Fig. 5, by means of which a sheet of glass is first cut into " ranges," and then each range chopped up into squares. The gauge is held in the right hand, and the straight-edge in the left hand is adjusted by means of the gauge—the notch being placed against the edge of the glass, and the point of the gauge against the straight-edge —until exactly parallel with the edge of the sheet. In chopping up the ranges a set-square is substituted for the straight-edge. In cutting the gauge from a piece of thin

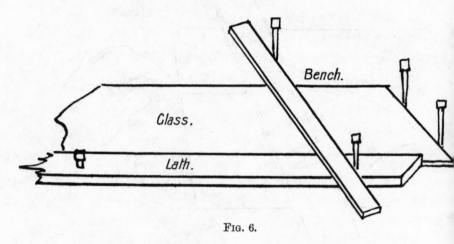

FIG. 6.

lath allowance has to be made (about $\frac{1}{8}$ inch) for the width of the block of the diamond.

There is also the bench gauge, shown in Fig. 6, an arrangement of laths to guide the sheet of glass and nails against which to set the straight-edge. This gauge is most useful for diamond-shaped quarries in which the angles are not right angles.

Considerable use is also made of moulds cut from stout cartridge paper. The outlines of the working drawing are transferred to the cartridge by means of carbon paper which is then cut to the various shapes, allowance being made for the heart of the lead. To avoid going over the ground twice, which is necessary with an ordinary knife or scissors, double-bladed knives and scissors are sometimes used. Of these the latter are quickest and easiest in use, but afford no adjustment for different thickness in the heart of the lead, whereas in the double-bladed knife the two blades can be set farther apart by the introduction of paper or tinfoil between them and secured by a set-screw. With this knife the paper is cut upon a piece of plate glass, and some dexterity is required to make both cuts without going over the ground a second time. An absolutely clean cut is necessary: any ragged edge will interfere with the passage of the diamond. The principal advantage in using these is to be found when cutting elaborate designs, geometrical or otherwise, where a number of pieces are required to one pattern, though they are sometimes called in even where there is no repetition to assist workmen who are not adepts at freehand cutting. They are sometimes useful to a slight extent in picking out the particular parts of variegated or streaky glass most suitable for certain effects, though for this purpose sheet glass patterns are very much better, for whereas the paper hides the very part which is required the sheet glass shows it clearly. When the sheet glass pattern is in the desired position its outline is marked upon the coloured glass by means of a pounce—a muslin bag filled with powdered chalk—and the cutting is done freehand. The sheet glass pattern is also used when ruby and other coloured glasses are too dark to enable the outlines of the drawing to be seen through them.

The freehand cutting of dark glasses can be rendered considerably easier by substituting for the wooden top of the bench a piece of stout plate glass with a mirror beneath it set at an angle of 45 degrees, or any other more suitable, to reflect the light upwards through it. The cutline drawing, generally of tracing paper or tracing cloth, is laid upon the plate, and the coloured glass upon the drawing. The reflected light from below makes it possible to cut all but the very darkest of antique glasses quite easily.

CUTTING.

Generally speaking, freehand cutting is the speediest and most economical for all work where there is no repeat—the man who requires paper patterns for one light is a poor workman, though the fact must be admitted that with lozenge and other rough glasses the guidance afforded by the edge of the paper pattern is well worth having even to a good man, and will sometimes save a great deal of waste through breakage.

FIG. 7.

The way of holding the diamond for cutting is illustrated in Fig. 7. It is not held like a pen or pencil, but between the first and second fingers and the thumb, flat places being cut upon the handle to accommodate the forefinger and thumb. The block in which the stone or "spark" is set is pivoted upon the handle and may be rotated through an angle of some 40 degrees. The advantage of this is to be found, sometimes in the cutting of intricate curved shapes with a paper pattern, sometimes in splitting up long ranges with a straight-edge, as it allows the hand to turn slightly without affecting the cutting direction of the diamond.

In cutting with the diamond the particular angle at which each individual stone must be held has to be learned by experiment, the sound and appearance of the cut being the tests by which it may be judged. The sound produced at a wrong angle is a decided scratch, and the mark left by the stone will look like a scratch—the sound produced at the correct angle by a good diamond is of a peculiar ripping quality, which is quite distinguishable from a scratch, but many diamonds make hardly any sound when cutting well. The look of a good cut is rather difficult to describe —it is not nearly so white and visible as a scratch.

Fig. 8.

It is of course only on the surface, though sometimes it can be seen to sink slightly into the body of the glass, and in the case of very thin sheet glass may even go right through at once. In the case of a straight cut the glass can generally be broken off without trouble, but with curved and intricate shapes "tapping" becomes necessary. For tapping the diamond is held as shown in Fig. 8. The block of the diamond strikes the glass hammer-fashion on the back, following the line of the cut. Steady tapping is essential, and the weight of the stroke varies according to circumstances. With a good cut the fracture will follow with a

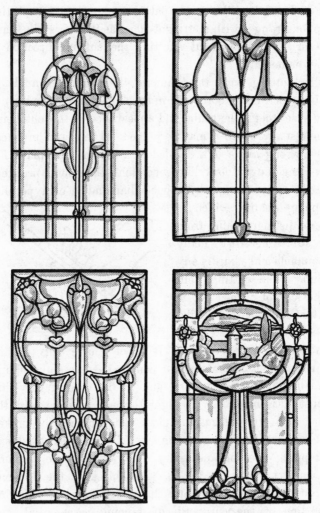

F<small>IG</small>. 9.—Designs for Leaded Lights, by Percy Jones.

jump at each tap, and in the case of a simple shape the pieces will fall apart. With more elaborate shapes the pieces will still be held together by their own dovetail and atmospheric pressure. Small marginal pieces may be broken off with the pliers, but notches in intricate shapes require special treatment. To get out the notch shown in Fig. 10 it will be necessary, after tapping the cut until the fracture has followed right round, to break up the glass in the bay by means of cross-cuts as indicated. These are again tapped, and if the tapping be continued will begin to break loose and fall away. Those following the line of the notch can then be broken off with the pliers, and the edge of the finished piece trimmed by means of "grozing." This is a peculiar action

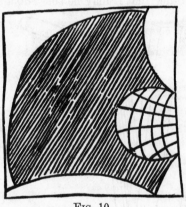

FIG. 10.

of the pliers, somewhat difficult to describe but easily acquired. The jaws of the pliers grip the edge of the glass rather loosely, and the handles are then worked up and down with a see-saw or pump-handle motion, chewing away the feathery and splintered edges. Sometimes it is sufficient merely to draw the pliers along the edge to break off the feather. Grozing is sometimes used for working into notches without the previous criss-crossing with the diamond, but the latter can be recommended as making a safer and surer job at the cost of little

extra time and trouble.   Allowance has always to be made
for the heart of the lead—from $\frac{1}{16}$ inch to $\frac{1}{8}$ inch—separating
the pieces of glass, and the regularity or irregularity of this
space will largely affect not only the neatness but even the
measurement of the finished work.

LEAD.

Lead used for this work must be as pure as possible in
order that it may be soft enough to bend easily around the

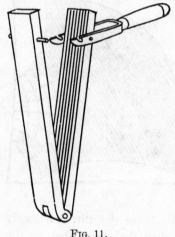

intricate shapes which are
sometimes used.   The presence of tin or other alloy
makes it too hard for this
purpose.   Pure lead is also
more likely to stand the
deteriorating effect of the
weather.   Formerly it was
the invariable practice to
cast the lead in a mould
(Fig. 11), the castings being
then passed through a vice
(Fig. 12) to produce the
finished section ready for

FIG. 11.

work.   Nowadays a very large proportion of the lead
used is turned out from hydrostatic presses in a manner
similar to lead piping, the same presses being used with
differently-shaped steel dies.   It is supplied by lead manufacturers to lead-light workers in two main forms—first,
as "calm" lead requiring to be passed through the hand
vice to obtain the finished section; second, as "window"
lead, ready for use.   In the first case, the calm can be

converted by means of the vice into many varying sections, special calms being supplied for extra sizes or sections. In appearance vice-drawn lead is distinguished from hydraulic-drawn by the marking upon the heart of the lead made by the milled wheels which force it through the vice, the hydraulic-drawn lead having a perfectly smooth heart. It may be further noted here that, whereas cast lead is produced in calms of about 18 inches long, hydraulic-drawn is turned out in coils which may contain 100 linear feet.

Hydraulic-drawn " window " lead is supplied by the manufacturers in no less than 150 different varieties, from $\frac{1}{8}$ inch to 1 inch wide, with " round," " flat," and "beaded" flanges, wide and narrow hearts, etc. One of the most notable firms in the trade is Messrs. Heaps, Arnold and Heaps, of Vicar Lane, Leeds, who have a very large selection of patterns,

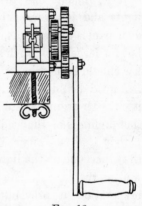

Fig. 12.

some of which are so unusual as to deserve the title of monstrosities, though all have their uses in certain circumstances. In spite of this variety, however, it is frequently found necessary to modify certain patterns to suit the requirements of customers, and it is always willingly done for a sufficiently large order.

There is a considerable demand at present for a steel-cored lead which will obviate the necessity for using iron saddle-bars and copper ties to stiffen the lights. There is no doubt these are somewhat unsightly, and in some respects the steel-cored lead is an improvement upon them. On the other hand the saddle-bar is sunk into the wood or stone frame to a much greater depth than the steel-cored lead, which goes no farther than the rebate, and so gives a greater amount of rigidity to the light. There is also a temptation to use up short lengths of steel-cored lead by joining them in the middle of a light, so defeating the very end they are intended to promote, and this little swindle is a very difficult one to detect. For comparatively small lights and for work subject to close inspection, such as door panels and screens, the steel core can be recommended, but for large work, such as church windows, etc., the saddle-bar should be used.

A good deal depends upon the treatment of the steel core itself. If ordinary steel be used it interferes with the thoroughness of the soldered joint, which ought not to be merely a surface affair, but should extend right through to the other side of the light, joining the heart of the lead as well as the flanges. As steel will not take solder without preparation, it prevents this penetration and causes the joint to be weaker than it would otherwise be. This objection is met by a special lead made by Messrs. Heaps, Arnold and Heaps and known as the " Dalton " lead (patented). The core in this case is tinned before insertion in the lead, and is therefore capable of being soldered with perfect freedom and making very strong joints. In the case of an outside lead the tinned steel core can be bent round the corner into the groove of the next piece and soldered there, thus making an extremely rigid fastening.

The advantage of using vice-drawn lead is that any particular section can be produced at a moment's notice, provided that the vice be equipped with suitable wheels and cheeks. As will be seen by Fig. 12, the vice is a comparatively small affair, but a considerable amount of power is necessary to work it. The vice itself is secured to a heavy bench by screws, the bench in turn being fixed to wall or floor. The size of the crank handle gives some idea of the resistance which has to be overcome—even with such a leverage it is sometimes necessary to introduce gearing to enable the machine to be worked by hand with reasonable ease. The end of the lead casting, or of a similar length of hydraulic-drawn lead, after being dipped in oil or smeared with tallow or other grease as a lubricant, is inserted between the two wheels, which, in turning, draw it in and force it between the cheeks, the wheels shaping the groove and milling the heart while the cheeks mould the flanges to a round, flat, or beaded form as desired. Wheels and cheeks to suit the different sections of lead are supplied with the machine and can be changed with very little trouble. The lead passes out from the vice into a long wooden trough which keeps it approximately straight— without this guide it would coil up and twist. In its passage through the vice it is stretched to about double its original length. Lead vices of various patterns with and without power gearing can be obtained from several manufacturers, notably from Messrs. Sharratt and Newth, of 43 and 44, Percival Street, Clerkenwell, E.C.

The use of vice-drawn lead also gives an opportunity of using up the scraps produced by cutting in the leading-up process. A gas melting pot will be found most convenient for melting these on account of the ease with which the heat can be regulated. The most important condition of successful work with the mould illustrated in Fig. 11 is to keep the mould well heated in order to prevent the molten lead from setting before it reaches the bottom of the grooves. It can be heated in the first place by laying it across the pot while the lead is melting. After the work is fairly begun the continual pouring in of hot lead will be sufficient to keep up the temperature. The molten metal is lifted from the pot with an iron ladle and poured into the mould. The ladle must be large enough to fill the mould at one pouring to ensure full length castings. When the casting has set it is removed by opening the mould and pulling it out with pincers. Occasionally, owing to slight slackness in the closing of the mould, thin webs of lead will be found adhering to the castings. These must be trimmed away with a knife before the castings are passed through the vice. The melting pot will also be found useful for the making of solder. The solder used for leaded lights should be of the " tinman's " variety —half lead, half tin. It can be obtained ready for use from the lead manufacturers, run out into thin strips which melt easily on application of the soldering bolt.

Leading Up.

Leaded lights are put together, or " leaded up," lying flat upon a bench. The working drawing is spread out and laths are nailed down to the rebate line along two sides of it. When the light is higher than it is broad the drawing should be placed so that its top comes at the worker's right hand and its bottom at his left. The outside lead is generally so arranged that about half of it will protrude from the rebate and show inside of the " sight

line." With a ¼ inch rebate, the most usual size, a ½ inch
flat lead is used so that its heart lies upon the sight line.
With a ⅜ inch rebate the ½ inch lead is also used, but the·
heart goes ⅛ inch beyond the sight line and only ⅛ inch is
visible. With a ½ inch rebate it is usual to use a ¾ inch
" unequal-heart " lead (with a groove nearly ½ inch deep on
one side and nearly ¼ inch on the other), the heart once
more coming upon the sight line, the broad flange going
into the rebate while the narrow flange
shows inside the sight line. Before
putting it into position the lead
must be slightly stretched in order to
straighten it. This is done by placing
one end of a length under the heel,
gripping the other end with the pliers,
and pulling upwards. A 6 feet length
of lead will stretch about 1 inch. Too
much stretching will weaken the lead,
destroy the smooth, close surface, and
even break it. An automatic device

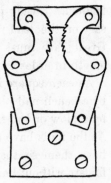

FIG. 13.

which admits of the stretching of much longer leads is
illustrated in Fig. 13. This is screwed permanently to the
bench at one end and is always ready for action. A length
of lead which formerly required a man at each end to
stretch it can by this means be manipulated by one man.
It is inexpensive and can be procured from Hetley's, of
Soho Square. The lead is then laid upon the bench and
the groove slightly opened on both sides with the lathykin
—on the one side to ensure its butting firmly against the
lath ; on the other to afford easy entrance for the glass.
This opening up is not so necessary in the case of round

or beaded lead as with flat. A lead having been cut to length and laid against each lath in this way, the pieces of glass are then inserted. In the case of a panel of plain squares these are first built up in the vertical direction of the light, working from left to right, the cross leads being cut rather shorter than the width of the squares of glass so that they will butt against the flanges of the upright leads. To cut the lead it must be laid on the bench with the heart vertical and the edge of the knife pressed through it chisel fashion. Steady pressure in a vertical direction is necessary or the lead will roll over and the heart be twisted. Great care must be taken to cut exactly to the correct length in order to make a neat and strong job.

As each square is laid in position it is temporarily fixed by a bench nail placed against the edge of it and driven in by a blow or two from the loaded handle of the lead knife. As the nails have to be constantly shifted, it is advisable to have them so that they can be easily withdrawn by the fingers without having to call the pliers into service. The notch in the blade of the lead knife mentioned above will come in useful for nails which are over firm. When the first column of squares has been built up in this way, a length of lead must be cut for the vertical line. It may be noted here that flat lead is generally used for the outside leads, but the others may be flat, round, or beaded. It is well to cut it to the correct length before proceeding to put it into position. The bent knife now comes into play. The nail is removed from the first square on the left, the point of the bent knife inserted under the flange of the first cross lead, and the glass by this means lifted from the bench just enough to allow the flange of the vertical lead to slip in between the glass and the bench. Each nail in turn is pulled out and put in again beyond the lead until the whole length is in position, and then the next row of squares is proceeded with. The reason for putting the cross leads in short pieces and the uprights in one piece is that any little inaccuracy in " running through " is more noticeable in a vertical line than a horizontal. When all the squares are in position the remaining two outer leads are put on and held in place by two more laths nailed down to the bench. Before nailing down the laths the measurements of the light should be checked—if it has worked too slack and is larger than it ought to be, it is sometimes possible to reduce the size slightly by hammering on the lath and so driving the squares closer together. Unless this is done carefully, however, there is a risk of the light buckling and the squares springing out of the leads, when the whole work has to be done over again. If it is on the small side it can be slackened out a little, but this should always be avoided as detracting from the strength and rigidity of the panel. The angles must also be tested with the set-square. Soldering can then be proceeded with.

Mention has already been made of the kind of solder employed. The fluxes used are various. Rosin is not to be recommended, because, though it makes a good job of the joint, it is exceedingly difficult to clean off. Palm oil is frequently used, but is very dirty. A " composition " candle rubbed on the joint before applying the solder makes the cleanest joint, but is a little slow in application. The same candle dissolved in raw linseed oil with the aid of heat gives excellent results. The mixture should be when cold about the consistency of thick cream, and can be applied rapidly and cleanly with a brush. If the joints are rubbed over with a piece of rag or cotton waste after soldering the bulk of the grease comes away at once. Muriate of zinc is generally used for applying copper ties after cementing when the lead has become blackened, but it is not necessary on clean lead.

The soldering bolt is a square-faced, not a pointed one. It will require to be "tinned" before using. To do this it must be heated to a working temperature, which must be judged by experience. A rough and ready test, which is most generally used, is to hold it within a couple of inches of the face. The heat at that distance should be just bearable. Another test is to apply to it a piece of solder which should melt quite easily. Overheating must be guarded against. Allowing a bolt to become red hot spoils the copper and pits the working surface so that it has to be filed down considerably to regain a level face. Gas bolts are provided with hooks by which they may be hung up during heating, as in that position the copper receives the full benefit of the heat from the flame. When the heat seems right the face is lightly rubbed over with a file to clean it. It is then rubbed on a piece of sheet tin with a little solder and grease until some of the solder adheres to the face of it, making it ready for action.

Neat joints can only be got by having the bolt at the right heat, by placing the face of it neatly on the joint and holding it firmly till the solder runs into place. Rubbing the bolt about on the joint only spreads the solder where it is not required and makes a clumsy, unsightly joint.

As soon as all the joints are soldered on one side the

laths can be removed and the panel turned over. This turning over is not quite so simple an affair as it might appear. In the present condition of the panel, soldered only on one side, it is ready to bend like a hinge at every lead line on the least provocation. It must be drawn forward with the right hand until the middle of it rests upon the edge of the bench. The farther side is then grasped with the left hand and raised. As the left hand rises the right must be depressed, the panel being supported also on the edge of the bench, upon which it swings see-saw fashion until it becomes vertical. In the vertical position it is comparatively safe from bending. It has then to be turned round, holding it as much as possible by the upper corners and letting it hang below the hands rather than above them. If it be set down without support it will at once collapse. The best plan is, immediately on lifting it from the bench, to lay it against a board or boards slanting against the wall. The drawing can then be lifted and the bench cleared before laying it down again to solder the back. The process of lifting must be exactly reversed in returning the panel to the bench. After the second side has been soldered it will be found that the panel has gained very greatly in stiffness, though it is still far from having the rigidity which is required of the finished article, and which is completed by the cementing process.

In lights of unusual size, such as long church windows, it is necessary to break them up into convenient sizes for handling. A leaded light should never be more than about 5 feet in its larger dimension, unless under exceptional circumstances. This breaking-up is accomplished by means of what is known as a " break-lead." The lower part of the light is finished in the usual way with a flat lead at the top of it. The flanges of this upper lead are then folded down upon the heart one over the other, or in some cases cut away altogether. The lower lead of the upper part is then placed in position, its flanges being opened up to allow the heart to come into close contact with the lead of the lower light. The construction then goes on as before, but in soldering these two leads are not connected, and so the light remains in two parts until it is fixed. In fixing, the flanges of the upper or riding lead are rubbed down into close contact with the lower lead and make a weatherproof joint which is farther strengthened by placing a saddle-bar against it. It will be evident that in cutting the glass special allowance has to be made for break-leads, as two hearts come together instead of only one.

CEMENTING.

The cementing of leaded glass is a process of the utmost importance, inasmuch as on it depends not only the rigidity of the whole, but also its ability to effectually resist the penetrative powers of wind and rain. The cement must be waterproof, of a tough and elastic, rather than a brittle, nature, and capable of adhering to both lead and glass. White lead would be an ideal material for the purpose but for its expense. The thick smudge collected in painters' workshops from the remains of paint of various kinds makes a good cement on account of the quantity of white lead which it contains. Putty powder, mixed with a little red lead and boiled linseed oil, is occasionally used. Ordinary glaziers' putty, softened with raw linseed oil to the consistency of very thick paint and coloured with lamp black to a dark grey, makes a good cheap cement, but of course the raw oil takes longer to dry than boiled oil. This, however, can be remedied by the addition of a small quantity of patent driers. Another recipe reads as follows:— Two parts of whiting to one part of plaster of Paris mixed with equal parts of boiled oil and turpentine. A little red lead will help to harden, patent driers will assist the drying, and lamp black will bring the colour right.

The actual details of application and cleaning off vary considerably, according to individual opinion. The following routine can be recommended as having been well tested. The cement is applied with a painters' hand brush which has been worn down to the condition of a "scrub." This will be found to have a good spring in its bristles and will work the stuff well in under the flanges of the lead without scratching the lead in the way some harder brushes do. The light is once more laid flat upon a bench—it is best to have a separate bench and indeed a separate room for cementing on account of the dust which flies about—and the cement well rubbed in, not merely painted on. It is brushed right over lead and glass and must be well rubbed into the corners, which are liable to receive less than their fair share : the test of good cementing is to work a stiff cement right through to the other side of the light. The light must be lifted from the bench occasionally to watch for this, and when the cement shows freely on the lower side the surplus can be cleaned off from the side under treatment. Some cementers have a trick of lifting the edge of a light from the bench and bending the whole thing slightly to and fro to work the cement through. This should be strongly objected to as weakening the work by stretching the leads and so giving more space to be filled by the cement. The cleaning is best done with a wisp of hay or a handful of rags or cotton waste which will remove the bulk of the stuff, but no effort should be made at this stage to thoroughly clean it all off. It is worth while now to dust the light over with whiting and rub this into the leads with the fingers, so stiffening the cement and helping to prevent its working through again from the other side. The light is then turned over and the cement brushed in on the other side. After the application of the whiting to the second side the light should be set against the wall—or rather against a sloping board—to harden before cleaning off, and allowed to stand overnight. It is then dusted over with clean, dry sawdust and rubbed with an ordinary scrubbing brush, which removes the film of oil and cement adhering to the glass and polishes up the leads, the mixture of whiting and sawdust making an admirable polish. The edges of the leads are then run round with a pointed stick of hard wood to clear out the corners and leave all sharp and clean. The panel must then be set aside for a few days to harden.

If the cement be too thin it will give a lot of trouble in cleaning off, running through from side to side, and will be found to ooze out after cleaning—the remedy is simply to make it stiff to begin with, and not to shirk the harder work of rubbing it through. When it has been allowed sufficient time to harden the stiffness of a well-made leaded light is really surprising as compared with its flabbiness when first lifted from the bench.

Where glass has been doubled—two glasses inserted into one lead—cement should never be used, on account of its

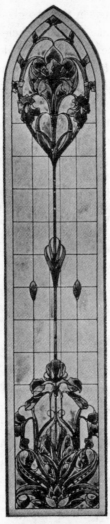

FIG. 14.—Design for Chapel Windows,
by Walter J. Pearce.

tendency to run between the two glasses and make blotches which are quite inaccessible for cleaning. In such cases stiff putty should be used and worked well under the flanges of the lead with the fingers. In the case of old painted glass which has been re-leaded, too, it is advisable to use putty, because the pigment, though possibly still satisfactory in appearance, may not be in a condition to stand the scrubbing entailed in cementing, and extra care must be taken in cleaning off, soft rags being substituted for the scrubbing brush. In the case of a hurried job, when time is not allowed for the necessary setting of the cement, putty is less likely to squeeze out during handling and fixing; but cement should always be used when possible, as being thinner it penetrates more thoroughly between lead and glass and makes more satisfactory work.

STOPPING-IN.

Repairs to leaded lights are made by means of " stopping-in." The flange of the lead surrounding the broken glass is carefully raised by inserting the face of the lead knife under it and levering it up all round, assisting this by cutting through the solder joints. The stopping knife is also useful as soon as the lead knife has made room for it, and with it the flange is turned up to a vertical position. Obviously this is an easier matter with flat than with round lead, but even with heavy round lead it can be managed with patience. The broken glass is removed, the new piece—cut perhaps a shade smaller than the old—is dropped in, and the lead turned down again and soldered off. The lead, except with a thin, flat lead, will naturally show that it has been interfered with, and care must be exercised to prevent its being quite spoiled. Where several pieces of glass are broken near the edge of the light, the best plan undoubtedly is to cut them all away and start with fresh lead and glass. The special value of stopping-in is that it enables small repairs to be made without removing the light from the window frame.

DOUBLE GLAZING AND PLATING.

Two devices known as "double glazing" and "plating" are occasionally used in leaded work to modify the colour of any particular piece of glass. Where a particular colour can be got in no other way, two pieces of glass are occasionally used in one lead, an extra wide heart being generally necessary to accommodate the thicker pieces of antique and slab glass. The mixture of wide-heart and narrow-heart lead is apt to look somewhat unsightly on the inside face of the light, but it is unavoidable when these heavy glasses are used, as they frequently require it even where there is no doubling. To use wide-heart throughout would not solve the difficulty—the heart of the lead must always be as narrow as the glass will allow to ensure strength and to hold the cement. The amount of wide-heart necessary is comparatively small, because only the darker glasses require it, and the colour effect gained by the quality of the thick glass is well worth striving for. A good instance of the value of double glazing occurs in the case of purple. A good purple glass is extremely difficult to obtain, whereas a very fair one can be got by doubling ruby with blue, and a really excellent one by combining gold pink ruby with blue, the combination affording a depth, quality, and life far beyond comparison with any pot metal or flashed glass.

"Plating" is not quite so legitimate and is generally only used to modify the colour of any piece of glass after it has been built into the light. A new piece of glass of suitable colour is superimposed upon the light, the new piece being first surrounded with a suitable lead. The outer flanges of this, being unnecessary, are cut away, and then the patch is soldered on to the face of the light. The appearance of this contrivance is not exactly ship-shape, being even more obtrusive and objectionable than the wide-heart lead, and is best avoided. It seems to be extensively used in America, three or four thicknesses being sometimes added.

FIXING.

The mode of procedure in fixing leaded glass varies according to whether the window frame is of wood, stone, or iron, and whether rebated or grooved. The easiest frame to fix glass into is undoubtedly a wooden one with rebate and beads. The panel must first be placed in position, and the positions of bars marked upon the woodwork. The panel is lifted out again and the holes cut. As round bars are most frequently used, the most convenient tools will be a brace and bit. Lights of less than a foot wide, where the use of such a tool would be impossible, do not require bars. In the case of flat or square bars a chisel must be used to cut the hole. The bar ought to go at least half an inch into the woodwork beyond the rebate, and so it is necessary to make the hole on one side an inch deep in order that the bar may slip into it, clear the wood at the other end, and then slip back again into the other hole. The holes having been cut, the rebate is "bedded" with putty, the panel placed in position and carefully

pressed home. The bars are slipped into their holes, and
the copper ties fastened round them. This is best done by
crossing the ends and twisting them up with pliers. When
the wire is close round the bar the twisted ends are cut
down to a length of about half an inch and bent downward
beneath the bar to give as neat a finish as possible. If the
tying of the wires be roughly or carelessly done there is
considerable risk of tearing them away from the soldered
joint. Putty which has squeezed out at the side on which
the beads are to go is scraped off, and the beads can then be
fixed, this being generally done by the joiner who has
made the framing. The putty which has squeezed out on
the reverse side ought not to be cut away till the beads are
fixed.

In a stone rebate the procedure is similar, except that a
mason's chisels will be required to cut the holes, and
mastic cement is used in place of putty. In long lights,
such as church windows, the joining of the panels as
described under the head of " Leading up " must be
attended to.

Stone grooves require special handling of the panels.
Sometimes where the groove is deep and the outer lead of
the panel small, it is possible to slide the panel to the full
depth of the groove, pass the free side clear of the stone,
bending the light a trifle if necessary, and then bring it
back to its correct position, as has already been described
in the case of bars. When the groove is shallower and the
outer lead is intended to occupy the whole, or nearly the
whole, of it, the matter is a little more difficult. In this
case, when the light is made up the heart of the outer lead
is arranged to come a trifle inside the sight line, so that

the outer flanges can be bent up at right angles to the face of light. It will then slip in between the mullions until it reaches its position. It has then to be held in position there, either by tying it up to the bars or, where there are no bars, by hand, until the flanges are flattened down into the groove. This will be found to be mostly fingerwork. Where there are two men on the job the two flanges are sometimes opened out one to each side, and the two men, one inside, the other outside the building, press against one another in flattening them down again, but the operation is quite commonly performed by one man, both flanges being turned to the same side, and being pushed back together. Pieces of ornamental tracery, trefoils, quatrefoils, etc., are frequently made in sections to facilitate fixing, the riding lead being used at the joints. Where metal casements are introduced they must be fixed along with the bars before the glass is put into place. Putty is used in fixing leaded glass into casements and metal frames generally. Holes should be provided in the "feather" of the frame, into which metal pins can be inserted to hold the glass in position. Wooden pegs are sometimes used for this purpose, but can hardly be regarded as satisfactory, though they may stand well enough if completely protected by the putty.

When using mastic cement in stone grooves, the mastic, which is a mixture of sharp sand, litharge, and slaked lime, and must not be confounded with gum mastic, is mixed with boiled linseed oil and a small quantity of putty. It is naturally of a very "short," friable nature, and the putty helps to make it more workable. Oil must be applied to the stonework to give the mastic a chance of adhering to it. Mastic sets very much more slowly than Portland cement, and there is less risk of breakage through changes of temperature to glass fixed with it. Mastic is therefore most suitable for use upon new work, but on old work— mullions of doubtful stability in old buildings, for instance— it is frequently advisable to use Portland cement in order that the whole may set as quickly as possible, before there is any chance of a gale of wind coming along and blowing the whole thing in.

The following two recipes for mastic cement may be useful where the mixture cannot be procured ready made·—

(1.) Quartz sand   ...   ...   60 parts
      Limestone ...   .   20 parts
      Litharge (monoxide of lead)   10 parts
      Linseed oil...   ...   ...   7 parts

Reduce all materials to fine powder before mixing with oil.

(2.) Powdered slaked lime   30 parts
      Sand   ...   ... $17\frac{1}{2}$ parts
      Litharge   ...   ... $1\frac{1}{2}$ parts

Knead to a stiff mass with $3\frac{1}{2}$ to 5 parts of old linseed oil, or linseed oil varnish may be used. Work thoroughly in a mortar with a pestle.

CALMS OF BRASS, ETC.

The use of brass calms in place of lead has recently been introduced, but does not seem to have met with any very favourable reception. It can be claimed in the favour of brass that it possesses great strength and that when nicely lacquered it has a very attractive appearance. Unfortunately, however, the lacquer is not everlasting, and the brass quickly blackens on exposure to the atmosphere, going wrong in streaks and patches which give it a very shabby appearance. The stuff is, of course, hard and does not bend so freely as lead; consequently the designs which can be carried out in it have less freedom than can be attained in lead. It has to be cut with a file or saw, and mitred at the joints; the joints are soldered, and the whole thing is then lacquered. There is no difficulty about the process or much variation from the ordinary practice in leaded light work. Indoors the lacquer would probably stand fairly well, but out of doors it does not. The repair of broken pieces of glass becomes a serious matter, too, as the rigid brass frame cannot be treated as lead is in stopping-in. There is no doubt as to lead being the best all-round material for work of this class. Pewter has been suggested and probably used in cabinet work and for door panels, etc. Its bright colour and capability of being polished are strongly in its favour, but against these is to be set its hardness—it consists of 80 per cent. of tin and only 20 per cent. of lead—which would prevent its bending with any freedom.

Zinc was in use for some years for quarries and simple geometrical patterns for church windows, but has entirely dropped out now. It made a very strong, rigid framework, but was very expensive, owing to the time which it took in working. The whole framework was built up, first, of T section calms, and soldered together. The glass was then dropped in and puttied as in wood or iron frames. It was wider than the average lead, and so stopped more light. It was more susceptible to the action of the weather.

Thousands of feet of such work have been pulled out and replaced with leaded lights.

DESIGN.

In designing for leaded glass there are two factors to be taken into consideration—the glass or coloured light, and the lead or darkness. Until some ten years ago the lead was looked upon, generally speaking, only as a sort of necessary evil—a mere divisional line between the pieces of coloured glass, and on that account to be kept as small and unobtrusive as possible. Even in geometrical patterns of light-tinted or white glass the only recognised value of the lead, from the point of view of design, was in defining the pattern. Then a reaction set in ; it was noticed that the lead itself might be utilised as an integral part of the design—that the black was useful as a foil to the light. At the same time the value of coloured glass unobscured by paint began to be more fully recognised, and traced and stained ornament to give way to bolder designs, in which the coloured glass was allowed to tell its own story with no help except that of the lead. The advantage of using heavier leads than the old $\frac{3}{16}$ inch and $\frac{1}{4}$ inch was recognised, together with the ornamental effect of using two or three contrasting widths of lead in one design. Under the old system the lead was a drawback and a nuisance—under the new it became a constant opportunity for the display of originality, ingenuity, and eccentricity. Glass manufacturers came forward with beautiful glasses which the older style of design gave practically no opportunity of using, while the newer style clamoured for them, and so the revolution was complete.

The craze for novelty has brought to light many devices which are worthy of preservation, a few of them being novel, but most mere revivals of mediæval practice. As examples of the latter may be quoted the use of pieces of sheet lead to supply patches of black, and the introduction of sheet copper, brass, and other metals, occasionally *repoussé*, to add interest to lead lights in doors of cabinets, etc. Certain enterprising firms have gone to the expense of patenting the use of copper, etc., in leaded lights, but they might as well have patented the use of lead. Mica, with its curious and varied colour and marking, has been used in place of glass to produce " quaint " effects—even such foreign substances as sea-shells, pebbles, and bits of coloured pottery have been pressed into the service. Out of all this unrest and feverish striving much unquestionable good has come. The eccentricities are disappearing, and a style of design thoroughly suited to the nature of the materials and taking full advantage of their opportunities is being evolved. At present there appears to be a standstill — the restless spirits find it impossible to go on discovering novelties, and eccentricity is giving way to sane and graceful design.

The severance between leaded and painted glass in ornamental work for domestic decoration is, however, much too marked. Without going back to the old style of work in which the transparent and translucent quality of the glass appeared to be quite a secondary consideration, there are opportunities of increasing the interest and value of leaded windows by using a certain amount of paint and stain—in painted outlines which will have greater freedom than lead lines because they do not require to join up to other lines, and which will add refinement because they may be so much thinner than the lead line—in patches of black and yellow and orange, which can be isolated because they do not require to be leaded in. It is along these lines that the next development in leaded glass design is likely to show itself. The worst obstacle at present is the prevailing craze for cheapness, though that may in a way be construed as an opportunity, as the class of people who look for glass of good design which shall be different from the cheap stuff of the everyday market will not object to a slight increase in price so long as they get what they want.

The constructional considerations which require attention in leaded light design are somewhat numerous. In the first place, every lead line must join up at both ends with other lines, as the lead is after all merely the dividing line between the pieces of glass. A minor exception to this can be made by allowing a short piece of lead flange to project an inch or two over the surface of a piece of glass and stiffening it with a liberal floating of solder, but it is seldom that such an evasion of the rules of construction is of any real service to the design, and as it is an evasion it ought to receive as little countenance as possible. The direction of lines has to be considered in relation to wind pressure and the banging of doors. In a design largely composed of radiating lines the radius leads will stretch in course of time, the panel will sag, and eventually the pieces of glass drop from the grooves; therefore large surfaces of radiating lines must be strengthened, by saddle-bars or steel-cored leads if necessary, but preferably by the introduction of other forms which will break up the radiating lines and tie the whole together. Shapes of pieces of glass have to be studied with regard to ease and even possibility of cutting. It is impossible for all practical purposes to cut, say, a figure 3 in glass, although very much more difficult things have been done, as *tours de force*, and the form must be modified or broken up accordingly. Pieces with narrow necks—dumb-bell and hour-glass shapes—are very liable to break across. Long narrow pieces and pieces with acute angles run the same risk.

Saddle-bars, which run a straight black line ruthlessly through the design, and which must never be more than about 18 inches apart, must be allowed for and so arranged that they shall help rather than hinder the design. (As has been mentioned elsewhere, it is possible to substitute for these steel-cored leads, but this is not always advisable, and in any case the steel-cored lead has exactly the same effect in cutting up the design.) The steadying effect of saddle-bars on an otherwise weak or loose design is sometimes remarkable. As an instance might be quoted a tall narrow lancet window in a church, filled with plain diamond quarries. The horizontal bars which break it at regular intervals appear at the first glance to mar the diagonal pattern, but a little consideration will show that the way in which they break up the monotonous quarries into panels is very useful. In some cases better effects could be obtained by a less regular spacing, giving the added interest of contrast in the size of the panels. Saddle-bars have been introduced in such windows set at the same angle as the quarries, but the effect is undoubtedly less happy, the hold of the bar in the stonework is not so good, and the extra length makes it less rigid. Bars are occasionally bent in order that they may avoid passing through some important feature of the design, but the practice is not a good one—as soon as a bar is bent its rigidity is tremendously reduced. The positions of the bars ought to be considered from the very first sketching out of the design and important features planned so as to be clear of them.

The introduction of ventilators which only occupy part of the opening has to be reckoned with, especially in church work. There are times when they might even be arranged to act to some extent as features in the design, or at least an effort might be made to lead up to them and support them in some way by means of the ornament, but this is seldom attempted.

In leaded lights for domes the designer is faced with a double difficulty—over and above all the usual considerations, which soon receive almost unconscious attention, there comes the task of accommodating the glass to the spherical form. Where the size of each individual panel is small in proportion to the whole of the dome it is sometimes possible to ignore the spherical shape during the making of the lights and bend them to the required curve when fixing. When the curve is more marked it is necessary to make a "saddle" of wood to the correct shape, and upon it to set out the drawing, cut the glass, lead up, and cement. Though this appears a somewhat formidable matter, it is well worth the extra work and attention in the accuracy which it ensures and the absence of the risk which would otherwise be run in bending the finished lights. In cases of extreme curvature it would, naturally, be impossible to bend a flat light to the saucer shape. The size of the pieces of glass must be accommodated to the acuteness of the curve when setting out the design in order to prevent breakage—it may be necessary where the design calls for large pieces of glass to call in the aid of the bending kiln.

Amongst minor considerations in design may be noted such a matter as size of squares. Of late years there has been a gradual increase in size of all pieces, the result being a lighter and more airy effect. The most popular size of " squares " at present is about 7 inches by 5 inches, but in large windows and in conjunction with well-designed ornament much larger sizes may be used. A "square" which is as broad as it is high does not look well in glass, though probably there is little but sentiment to account for this. A high narrow square always has more appearance of dignity than a squat one, and their usual position above the eye-level always seems to reduce the height by fore-shortening.

The use of arbitrary leads which do not help the design but are simply introduced · for constructional purposes should be avoided, as they proclaim in unmistakable and needless fashion the weak point of the material. The design ought to be so planned as to dispense altogether with such admissions of weakness. There are, of course, circumstances in which they are unavoidable, but it is generally possible to disguise them or work them into the design in some way. At the same time it is a mistake to allow pieces of glass to assume awkward or breakable shapes for the mere purpose of avoiding them, and there always comes a point when they must be frankly accepted.

Into the Ocean faint and far
Falls the trail of its Golden Splendour

FIG. 15.—Leaded Panel, designed by Wm. Aikman.

In the case of long sweeping curves which run through a mullion from one light of a window to another particular care must be taken, by setting out the drawings at the correct distance apart, to ensure that the curve is sweet and unbroken, as the success of an otherwise good design may be completely marred by a broken curve. Running a design through a number of lights must not be done in such a way as to completely ignore the mullions. They ought to be recognised as part of the design, and in addition to that each panel, while still forming part of the whole, ought to be as complete as possible in itself.

Not the least important part in designing for leaded lights is the selection of the glass both as to kind and colour. Under most circumstances it is advisable that the majority of the surface should be made up of light-tinted glasses of the less expensive kinds, such as sheet, rolled, or muffled. Sheet (or patent plate) will be necessary where a transparent background is wanted, while either rolled or muffled will answer for most positions where an obscure ground is asked for. Of these it should be noted that rolled is the quieter and more retiring in its effect, and therefore most suitable for backgrounds. Ornament in muffled glass on a background of rolled will stand out with satisfactory brilliance, whereas if the positions of the two are reversed the background will sometimes have the appearance of coming out in front of the ornament. "Flemish," in many respects an excellent background glass, is apt to fail occasionally in this respect, especially in direct sunlight. The *worst* glass for backgrounds, though it is frequently used as such, is "Venetian Lozenge." The brilliance and insistent regularity of its pattern make it stand out from everything near it, and the effect when it is used in large surfaces can only be described as vulgar in the extreme. Used in small pieces, as if it were valuable, it looks well, and is sometimes a very great acquisition to a smart design. "Ambitty" makes a splendid background when expense is not the first consideration, and it has the advantage, which is shared to some extent by muffled, of showing great variation in surface, so that it is possible by careful selection from different parts of a sheet to have a background composed of pieces gradating from very obscure at the bottom to almost transparent at the top—an effect which is sometimes desirable in screen work.

Antique glasses always look well either for background or ornament owing to their fine quality and are, except Opalescents, almost the only glasses which will give good ornament when used with a muffled background. Opalescents because of their brilliance and variegation are quite unsuitable for background work, but make excellent ornament, and can be used along with Antiques, though not exactly mixed with them. For instance, in the case of flowers and foliage, the flowers may be antique and the foliage opalescent, or *vice versâ*, but to use both glasses in the foliage would be courting failure. With flowers, of course, there is a little more latitude. It is quite permissible to put in, say, a conventional rose in opalescent, with a heart of Antique or Venetian, or an Arum lily with spathe of white antique and spike of yellow muffled. The juxtaposition of different textures of glass gives opportunity for some of the most successful effects obtainable in glass, even when colour is left entirely out of the question.

A brilliant and eminently satisfactory result can be

obtained in positions where colour is not desired by the combination of antique, muffled, Flemish, Venetian, and other glasses, all of pure white, though the success of it will depend very largely on the proportion of each used and the way in which they are contrasted.

As to combinations of colour, no suggestions can be made —that is a matter for the artistic taste and feeling of the designer. But with regard to colours available one may point out that in the cheaper glasses generally the only satisfactory colours, except light tints, are greens and yellows, and in the case of rolled cathedral a few blues. For browns and reds one must turn to antiques; for ruby to antique, opalescent, slabs, etc.; for quiet and subtle blues to antiques; for purples to slabs and double glazing. A natural result of this is seen in the great preponderance of yellows, greens, and light tints in work of the cheaper class. For backgrounds warm tints are generally more acceptable than cool tints—they suggest sunshine, and a staircase or hall glazed with them leads one to go to the door looking for the sunshine (possibly only to find overcast sky and rain, but still feeling thankful that things look so much more cheery indoors than out).

CHAPTER III

STAINED GLASS

THE term "Stained Glass" is an exceedingly unsatis-
factory one, insomuch as that it can be taken as conveying
several different meanings. In its most general sense it
includes many different processes, the most notable of
which would be exemplified in a complete memorial window
with figure and ornamental work; in a more limited sense
it is occasionally applied to *coloured* glass used in the production of such a window and for other general purposes—
it is sometimes applied to glass, white or coloured, painted
with metallic pigments and fired in a kiln—and in its most
limited sense to glass, originally more or less white, which
has been treated with yellow stain prepared from silver and
known to glass-workers as "*stain*." It is also occasionally
used as including leaded lights, but these are now fortunately recognised under their own specific name and so
simplify matters to some extent. This arrangement sug-
gests two classes, leaded lights and stained glass, the
latter being understood to contain all glass which is *painted*
instead of or in addition to being leaded. Coloured glass is
best described as coloured, unless any special definition,
such as antique, opalescent, slab, etc., can be given.

Having narrowed it down so far, we yet find that our
term will include a very great variety of work—elaborate
figure windows, simple devices on leaded quarries, Gothic

grisaille, Renaissance arabesques, elaborate enamel work, such as that of the seventeenth century Swiss workers, large rough cast plates for skylights with painted and stained designs. But after all the term glass painting is perhaps the best in this connection, that being the term generally in use in the trade.

The reader may be assumed to be beyond that dangerous state of knowledge in which people ask " Do you paint glass with oil or water-colour? "—to be aware that in nine cases out of ten the different colours of a window represent so many separate pieces of glass joined together by means of bands of lead, and that the only painting upon it is in the form of monochrome outline and shading, which assists the lead outline in defining the design.

The various steps in the production of a large painted window are as follow :—First, the coloured sketch, generally to a scale of one inch to a foot, in which a miniature representation of the design is given, and which is used as a reference and guide at all stages of the work ; second, the cartoon, a full-sized drawing in monochrome (black lead, charcoal, or water-colour), giving complete details of lead lines, painted outlines, and shading. Generally, for convenience, separate drawings are made for figure and ornamental portions. Third, the cutline drawing, which is traced from the cartoon on to tracing linen and shows the lead line only, in lines about $\frac{1}{8}$ inch wide, representing merely the heart of the lead. This naturally gives the exact shape of every piece of glass in the window and is used by the cutter in cutting the glass, from which fact it takes its name. The glass, when cut, is passed on to the painter, the ornamental portions frequently going to one man who specialises in ornament, the figure portions to another whose speciality is figure work. Occasionally this subdivision is carried so far as to call in a third man who does nothing but "flesh" (heads, hands, and feet), but this extreme is best avoided. Having been painted, the glass is fired in the kiln, once or oftener, as may be necessary, and is then passed on to the lead-worker, who puts the pieces together with the lead calms. Cementing follows, and the window is then ready for fixing in position.

PIGMENTS.

As cutting, leading, and cementing have been already fully dealt with under the heading of Leaded Lights, it only remains for us here to examine the process of painting and firing. The pigment with which the painting is done is a fusible glass in a finely-powdered condition mixed with metallic oxides which supply the colouring matter, or, rather, the opaque element. Its composition varies greatly, iron, manganese, cobalt, and copper all being used for colouring, while the flux also varies in fusibility. Its melting point must necessarily be just a little lower than that of the glass on which it is to be used, but the difference between various makes of colour in this respect is considerable. The importance of this matter lies in the fact that it largely affects the permanence of the pigment. With a soft colour fusion is attained before the glass has become sufficiently softened to allow the colour to sink into the surface and become really part of it. If firing is stopped at that point the colour has only a superficial hold upon the glass and is in no sense permanent. If firing be carried beyond that point the colour loses its density and fails in its object, which is to prevent the passage of light through the glass. The fact that the colour shows a glossy surface is not, then, sufficient to indicate that it is fixed and permanent. It is necessary that the glass itself should show signs of approaching fusion. Colours, therefore, which fuse at too low a temperature should be avoided. The presence of borax in any colour will cause it to flux at a very low temperature, and it is occasionally added to glass colour to ensure " a good gloss," but just on that account colours containing it should be rigidly banned as having no degree of permanence. It used to be the practice for glass painters to make their own colours, which had the advantage that the composition of the pigment was exactly known ; but even that did not ensure permanence, as advantage was sometimes taken of the knowledge to obtain a well-glazed surface without sacrifice of density, but at the expense of permanence. Nowadays a few painters still make their own colours with more or less success.

Within recent years chemical analysis of samples of painted glass whose pigment has stood the test of hundreds of years' exposure to the atmosphere has enabled manufacturers to produce colour which can be relied upon as permanent, so there is no longer any reason for painters to waste time and risk failure by experimenting. The colours which are at present most popular among glass painters are the Permanent Vitreous Colours produced by Messrs. Heaton & Son, of 19, Berners Street, London, W. They are generally understood to be the most reliable pigments on the market, and include a red tracing colour, two or three shading browns, a good black, etc. Of these the tracing colour is most generally useful, and by many people is used for shading also, but on pure white glass it is rather "brick-like" in tone, though this defect is corrected to a great extent on greenish whites. The browns are not open to this objection, and are very satisfactory otherwise. All these colours are finely ground, work well under the brush, and require a high temperature to fire them, in fact, a temperature at which soft glasses, such as some antique greens, run a risk of losing their transparency and even their shape. They lose density somewhat in firing, but that would seem to be unavoidable in glass colours, and certainly their loss is less than in other colours of more doubtful antecedents. This loss is, of course, allowed for in painting.

Amongst other manufacturers of colours may be noted Messrs. Hancock & Co., Worcester,—who, in addition to tracing and shading colours, make a fine range of enamel colours and stains—Messrs. Wenger & Co., Hanley, and Messrs. Harrison & Co., Hanley.

These pigments do not in any way affect the *colour* of the glass ; they only add shadow and outline to the outline and colour already provided by the lead and glass, giving finer and more accurate definition to the design ; they "stop out" a certain amount of the light which would otherwise pass through the glass. *Enamel* colours, on the other hand, do add colour to white glass, but at the expense of trans-parency. The colour does not become part of the glass, but merely lies on the surface in an opaque film, giving an effect very similar to what might be produced by coloured paper. The great bulk of seventeenth century stained glass was painted with enamel colours, the amount of pot metal in it being very small, and is notable chiefly for its heavy, sombre appearance, which is the reverse of glassy, and secondly for the very capable technique of the painting. This heavy opacity, then, is inseparable from the use of enamel colours. In what may be looked upon as the Golden Age of stained glass—from the twelfth to the four- teenth centuries—they were never used, and a window of the fourteenth century is as far removed from one of the seventeenth in the matters of depth and quality of colour and transparency of effect as is the North Pole from the South. There is no doubt as to which is the finer and nobler, and it is certain that future practice will follow the older lines.

Enamel colours have had a great vogue in domestic work for the painting of "centres" with birds, landscapes, etc., in more or less realistic colouring. From an artistic point of view there is nothing to be said for these, and, except as regards permanency, they would have been as well or better done on paper. However, there is still a demand for them in certain quarters, though it has been tremendously shaken recently by the production of "up-to-date" designs in cheap lead lights. Enamels may be used in a fairly legitimate way to enhance the effect of stain in painted arabesque designs on white glass, such as rolled and muffled, where the large amount of clear background will make up for some loss of transparency in the ornament.

The silver stain which has been mentioned above stands out as a curious exception from other glass colours. It is really a *stain*, the silver of which it is composed penetrating the surface of the glass and producing a perfectly trans- parent colour with no opaque layer upon the surface. Its usefulness is naturally restricted to pale tinted glasses—

whites, pale greens, and light blues. Pure whites are generally rather hard, and do not take the stain very readily, so it has to be applied fairly strongly on them; greenish whites stain very well, but when the green becomes too marked the stain loses its transparent golden quality and becomes brownish and muddy. On pale pot metal blues it is sometimes possible to use stain, but the result is never very clear. On flashed blue, however, a very good effect can be obtained, as the stain works well on the white body of the glass, while the blue flash can be modified or removed by means of acid, giving a range of colour from blue through green and yellow to white. This combination is occasionally made use of to introduce conventional landscapes as backgrounds to figure subjects, and has a very good effect, and it has the additional advantage of being one of the most legitimate and most interesting "dodges" in the craft.

Yellow stain can be procured from colour manufacturers ready for use, but most glass painters prefer to make their own and modify it to suit the particular work in hand. The active principle, as already mentioned, is silver, which is combined with various earths to reduce its strength and to afford a convenient means of applying to the glass. On being subjected to heat in the kiln the silver combines with the surface of the glass, while the earth remains unaffected and can be brushed off afterwards. The process of manufacture is quite a simple one. From a number of recipes the following two may be taken as representative. In the first, 1 oz. of pure metallic silver is melted with 2 oz. of sulphur and 2 oz. of black antimony in a crucible. The molten metal, on being poured into water, disintegrates into a powder, which is then dried and mixed with three times its weight of Venetian red (dry powder) and ground in water until fine enough for use, when it can be again dried, if it is desired to mix it with turpentine. If it is intended to be used with water, all that is now necessary is the addition of gum arabic. The melting of the silver can be very conveniently accomplished by means of a very neat little gas furnace and crucible, to be obtained from Messrs. Griffin & Co., Ltd., London. It consists of a Bunsen burner with two cylindrical jackets, the inner of plumbago, the outer of fireclay, and a long chimney of sheet iron to induce greater draught. A sliding iron collar on the shaft of the burner supplies a means of regulating the air supply to suit the gas pressure, and two small crucibles, one of fireclay, the other of plumbago, complete the outfit.

In the second recipe, the silver is reduced by the action of nitric acid. The silver is placed in a glass vessel, such as a pickle jar, pure nitric acid poured over it, and water added. The chemical action is allowed to continue until the silver is entirely dissolved. A handful of common salt is then thrown in, and the metal is precipitated as chloride of silver. The acid is now poured off and the precipitate washed with repeated additions of hot water. The water is poured in, time is given to allow the silver to settle, and then the water is poured off again, care being taken not to pour off any of the silver with it, as a great deal of the silver may very easily be lost in this way. About half a dozen washings ought to be sufficient. Yellow lake is then added— two of lake to one of silver—and the mixture ground.

The first of these makes a good stain for fairly hard glasses and for " floated " work ;   the second is more suitable for church window work and for soft glasses generally. It also has the advantage that, on account of its greenish-yellow colour, it is rather easier to judge the strength with which it is applied and consequently its appearance when fired. Stain is generally mixed with turpentine and fat oil or japan gold size, but for " floating " purposes, which are seldom required nowadays, with water and a very little gum. Floating was mostly used on the old " kelp " glass, on which it was possible by this means to obtain a deep orange-red stain, which at times vied with flashed ruby for depth and richness of colour. The glass had to be laid down perfectly level, a strong stain mixed with plenty of water and laid on—*floated* (there is no other word for it)—with a round camel-hair wash-brush, fully charged, in such a way as to leave no possibility of brush marks. A slight cloudy variation was sometimes noticeable in the finished work, but at its best the colour was perfectly flat and equal, perhaps a little too much so. As "kelp" glass is practically unobtainable nowadays, this process is seldom called for.

VEHICLES.

In practice glass colours are mixed with various vehicles according to circumstances and individual preference. Fat oil of turpentine, produced by exposing spirits of turpentine to the air, with a covering to exclude dust, for some weeks in order to allow of evaporation of all but the least volatile oil, is one of the best binders. The colour is first mixed with a palette knife in spirits of turpentine to a stiff, short paste; then the fat oil is added, the test as to quantity of fat being the time required for the colour to dry flat. If it dries flat in less than, say, ten minutes, it will not flow freely enough from the brush to allow of good clean brush work—it has not sufficient fat; if it has too much fat, it will "fry" in the kiln during firing and leave the lines full of minute pin-holes, will produce a grey instead of a black effect. In its best condition it will dry flat in from half an hour to an hour. Colour deficient in fat will not work freely enough to produce good clean lines and rapid work. Spirits of turpentine are used as necessary for thinning. Colour made up in this way will of course grow "fatter" from day to day as more turpentine is added and evaporated, and it may be necessary to "flatten" it by the addition of dry colour.

Japan gold size may be used in place of the fat oil. In this case less turpentine will be required, as the gold size is so much thinner than good fat oil, and a larger quantity of gold size than of fat oil. It will be found that the colour will dry flat with a much larger quantity of gold size than of fat oil. The freedom in working is not quite so great, and there is again the risk of frying, especially if the colour be piled on too thickly. Venice turpentine may also be used in the same way. Shading colour is sometimes mixed with oil of tar. Spike oil of lavender is occasionally used when applying turpentine colour over water colour, in a manner which will be explained later.

In some respects water has distinct advantages over turpentine. Colour made up with it dries more quickly, and can be handled or packed sooner; water colour which has dried on the palette is more easily worked up again than turpentine colour; and, finally, it affords opportunities for applying outline and shading with one firing which cannot be had with turpentine. Along with the water may

FIG. 16.—Leaded Panel in Mixed Glasses.
Wm. Pape, Leeds.

be used treacle, sugar, glycerine, or gum arabic as binding. The gum arabic produces very different results in working from the other three, which are all very similar in their nature. Colour prepared with either of these works very similarly to fat turpentine colour. Too little sugar makes the colour drag; too much will make it fry. Colour prepared with gum is very different: it works more loosely and freely, is less suave and clinging, a little less easy to handle perhaps for a beginner, but capable of great speed and freedom in practised hands. (This applies, of course, to tracing or outline work.) Again, there is the same difficulty as to quantity, but in this case there is no tell-tale gloss to show the presence of too much gum. It must be tested with the scrub. A small quantity is stippled or brushed thinly on to a piece of glass and allowed to dry. If then it can be not too easily removed with a hog-hair scrub, the quantity of gum will be about right for tracing colour; for shading colour the quantity of gum should be smaller. In this case the scrub ought to leave clean brush marks, without any trace of drag or lumpiness. Colour which is too hard to be removed by the scrub will inevitably fry when applied in the thickness necessary for a solid line. Gum arabic bought in the lump, of the purest quality, and dissolved in water, is the most reliable variety, but it is being ousted to some extent by the powdered form. The powder has the great advantage of not requiring to be dissolved beforehand. The colour can be worked up in water with the palette knife and ground with the muller if necessary; then a pinch of the powdered gum can be sprinkled over it with the fingers, dissolving as it is worked into the colour.

The gum colour would appear to be best and most practical on the whole, because it is simplest and most adaptable, besides giving the advantage of one-fire work.

Palettes for glass colours are generally pieces of obscured plate glass about 9 inches square. One is reserved for each pigment in use; and to store them in small space, protect them from dust, and save the loss of colour resulting from inadvertently turning a wet palette up on edge against the wall, as is frequently done, it is well to have a small cupboard. This should measure 9 inches square inside, and a height suitable to number of palettes in general use; it should have bearers on either side about 1½ inches apart, upon which the palettes can rest, and a door as nearly as possible air-tight. The exclusion of air will help to keep the colours from drying, and so save a little time and trouble when beginning work each morning. At all times it should be remembered that it is better to work with a small quantity of colour, and to make up fresh as often as necessary rather than to use old and stale stuff, which will not fire so well or give such good results. There is a tradition amongst glass painters that old colour works best. Probably it does on the palette and on the glass, but the opinion of the colour-makers is that freshly made-up colour fires best. The moral is that colour should not be merely *mixed* with the water or turps, but well and carefully ground.

Tools.

One or two palette knives will be wanted (it is well to have a separate knife for stain) with blades about 6 inches long, or longer for large batches of colour. Glass mullers for grinding the colour are useful, though the old-fashioned granite muller is considered by some people to be more efficacious. Colour as it is turned out nowadays by manufacturers is generally in good working order, but it cannot be ground too fine. Old glass painters have vivid memories of weary hours in their boyhood's days which are spared to the present generation. The mullers will be required specially for grinding stain. A hand-rest, consisting of a piece of wood 3 inches wide, $\frac{3}{4}$ inch thick, and from 2 feet to 3 feet long, supported on a block at either end to raise its upper surface $2\frac{1}{2}$ inches to 3 inches above the bench, will be useful, although some workers dispense with it altogether. For the beginner it is absolutely necessary, and for good clean tracing it is always an advantage.

For tracing several " tracers " of camel or sable hair and of various sizes are required. The kind of hair is a matter of individual taste and experience, and no hard and fast rule can be laid down with regard to it. For shading the outfit is a little more comprehensive. A flat camel-hair wash-brush in tin about 2 inches wide, a badger-hair softener about 4 inches wide, two stipplers, large and small (these are specially made for glass painting by Messrs. Hamilton & Co. and other makers), and a number of " scrubs " of various sizes are wanted. The latter are hog-hair brushes of the type commonly used for oil painting. Some of the shorter patterns will do in their original condition, but are rather lacking in body. The most useful scrubs are made from a longer-haired pattern by cutting them down. Roughly speaking, the length of the hair should be a trifle greater than the width of the tin (in flat brushes, which are the most useful kind). To trim down the roughly cut ends the brush must be rubbed upon

sand-paper, holding it in the usual way and drawing it
over the surface of the paper as if painting. As soon as
the hair is restored to something like its original appearance the brush is ready for work. In addition to these, a
goose quill pointed like a pen, but not split, is sometimes
useful, together with a needle point set in a wooden handle.
Camel-hair brushes of goose and swan size set in quills
are used for stain, and are also useful occasionally for
strengthening shading with turpentine colour over water
colour. Brushes once used for stain must never be used
for any other colour, as the stain would destroy the
other pigment in firing. It is partly on this account that
stain is never spoken of as *colour*, but kept apart by its
own distinctive name. A badger softener is sometimes
useful for stain, and should be kept for that purpose to
avoid contaminating colour with stain; but, as these
are expensive brushes, many people are content to use one
badger for all purposes, merely taking the precaution of
thoroughly washing it at each change. This can be done
with soap and water, and drying can be rapidly done by
twirling the brush between the palms of the hands. As
the brush continually accumulates colour in the course of
use, frequent washing is necessary to keep it clean, and
therefore in a condition to produce a fine matt.

PAINTING.

Tracing or outlining is the first process in glass painting.
The drawing or cartoon bearing the required design is
placed upon a bench immediately in front of a good window,
north light whenever possible. The hand-rest already

described will be required. The palette, with colour already prepared, pot for water or turpentine, as the case may be, palette knife, and tracing pencils, are placed to the right of the drawing. After the glass has been cleaned of any grease or dirt it is laid flat upon the drawing, when, except in the case of exceptionally dark colours, the outline of the design will be more or less visible through it. The hand-rest is placed bridge fashion across it to support the hand. The tracer is *well* filled with colour, and the lines of the drawing are traced upon the surface of the glass. The beginner will experience a curious difficulty in that, with his eyes focussed on the drawing, below the glass, he will find the pencil point come into contact with the glass sooner than he expects and make a blob of colour instead of beginning the line neatly and cleanly. A little experience will obviate this. A firm, clean, solid black line—solid, that is, when held up between the window and the eye—must be striven for. The colour will be reduced in density by the firing in the kiln, and allowance must be made for this reduction. Care must be taken also not to pile on the colour too thickly, as that would cause frying even when the composition of the colour was correct. It is well when "filling in" bits of solid black to avoid piling the colour over lines which have already dried. In other words, do not trace all outlines first and fill in afterwards, but fill in as you go along before the outlines have dried. The colour on the palette must be freshly stirred up with the knife from time to time to keep it in good working order, more water or turpentine being added as required. Lines which are ragged on the edges or thicker than required may be trimmed down with a needle or hard wood point, but this dodge is apt to encourage slovenly tracing and should be indulged in as little as possible.

When working with deeply-coloured antique glasses it is sometimes impossible to see the lines of the drawing through them. This difficulty is met by tracing the lines first on a piece of clear sheet glass. This sheet is then placed over a piece of white paper and tilted, desk fashion, the dark glass being laid upon the slope, which has, in the case of very dark stuff, to be fairly steep. If the glass will not remain in position it can be held by a dab of beeswax. It will then be found that the light reflected from the white paper will enable the lines on the clear sheet to be followed with ease on the antique glass.

Painted glass, except under special circumstances, is always fixed with the painting towards the interior of the building. This being so, it is advisable when using rolled, muffled, and similar glasses to paint upon the rougher side, thus allowing the smoother side, which will afford less hold to dirt, to be turned outwards.

A certain amount of shading can be done at this stage by brushing-on. If the same colour be used as for tracing, care will be necessary to avoid disturbing the outlines. If turpentine colour be used for shading over water-colour, the risk of disturbance is very slight, but *vice versâ*, especially if the turpentine colour have gold size as a binder, it is much more considerable, the line sometimes sliding away bodily in pieces half an inch long. Moreover, the water-colour has a peculiar trick of receding from the oil-colour, producing a light, cloudy fringe on either side of the black line and entirely preventing any chance of obtaining a flat effect. All painting over unfired lines must be done smartly and without hesitation or niggling. The touches of the shading pencil may be modified, softened, or graded to some extent by using a badger softener, but at increased risk of disturbing the line. Whenever possible the touches of the brush ought to be allowed to retain their original character, which should be clean, brisk, and rather " blobby " than otherwise. A few such touches at this stage may supply all that is necessary in the way of shading for some of the lighter Renaissance designs, and the cleaner they can be pencilled on and the less the badger is used the better and smarter will be the effect. Even where the work is to be stippled over afterwards it is frequently useful to put in these touches in order to gain strength in particular places, and "pencil shading " is well worth a good deal of practice.

The majority of shading on glass is done by " brushing-out." The colour is first spread equally over the whole surface in a matt or stipple, and the high lights and half-tones are then scrubbed out, leaving the shadows untouched, something after the fashion of the scraping process used in mezzotint. To produce a good matt, the colour—water and gum : turpentine is useless for this work—must be laid on as equally as possible with a camel-hair flat brush, and then smoothed with a badger softener. The handling of the badger requires a great deal of practice. The brush must be held very lightly but firmly, and so used that only the delicate ends of the hair are allowed to touch the glass, across which they are swept in every direction to smooth out the wet colour and obliterate all trace of brush marks. If the badgering be continued too long, the colour will dry very rapidly and, in a half-dry state, be very easily scratched by the badger-hair. Depth of colour is very difficult to judge—it ought to be the depth of the darkest shadow. The colour will look slightly darker when dry than when wet.

For a stipple the colour is brushed on with a flat brush in the same way, and afterwards worked over with the stippler. This is handled in quite a different way from the badger, being held at right angles to the surface of the glass all the time and "dabbed"—not brushed—against it. The stippler has to be prepared for work by dabbing it over a small quantity of wet colour on the palette—if it were applied dry to the wet colour on the glass it would simply mop it up. When it will lift no more of the wet colour it is ready for use. For a rough stipple a large brush and comparatively wet colour are required, for a fine stipple a smaller brush and drier colour. A very good fine stipple is obtained by means of the badger, by first producing a more or less smooth matt and then stippling it over with the badger. In this case the badger collects sufficient wet colour during the matting process to prepare it for the subsequent stippling. Owing to the different ways in which they are used, badgers and stipplers require very different treatment. The badger, as already stated, should be frequently washed in water, occasionally with a little soap, to keep it free from colour and enable it to produce a clean, smooth matt. The stippler, on the other hand, ought not to be washed. By constant use it builds up a number of dry blobs of colour on the points of its stiff bristles, by means of which it gives the peculiar character to the coat of colour upon the glass. (This applies more particularly to church windows for distant effect.) An old glass painter is dreadfully concerned when you handle his stippler lest you should, by your ignorance or carelessness, knock off any of the blobs.

We now have in the matt a perfectly smooth, even coat of colour without texture—in the stipple a coat of spotty texture which has been irreverently compared with smallpox. The matt is worked upon with "scrubs" only—on the stipple the fingers are also used and produce an effect which the "scrub" cannot give. The scrubbing out of the colour to produce the light and shade effect has to be gone about with some care, as in case of removing too much colour it is necessary to renew the matt or stipple and start afresh. Generally speaking, it is best to go for breadth of treatment, taking out the half-tones as broadly as possible, but keeping everything at first on the dark side and coming finally to the high lights. The high lights will be found to have a peculiar effect of expanding when viewed from a distance owing to the diffusion of the light after it has passed through them. On this account there is a considerable risk of getting the high lights too broad and open, which must be guarded against by opening them up very gradually and frequently viewing the work from a distance. The scrub must be held lightly but firmly, and worked more or less in one direction with respect to folds of drapery, surfaces of ornament, etc., so as to produce some recognisable effect of technique. The stiff bristles of the brush produce a number of fine parallel scratches in the colour which can be made to follow the direction of any form in the design, and the appearance of the work will largely depend upon the use which is made of the opportunity thus given.

The stipple, whether it be worked by scrub or fingers,

has the property of retaining its texture throughout—you may work till you have effaced it from the glass, but you cannot make it look smooth. The chief advantage which the stipple has over the matt is that it never looks so dead and heavy. A comparatively thin matt seems to stop all light, while the spottiness of the stipple allows a certain amount of light to pass even through the strongest shadows, and so preserves the glassy effect. Consequently it is advisable, whenever possible, to finish stippled work in one working: in going over it a second time even with the stippler some of these light spots are bound to be clouded over and rendered opaque. When it is necessary to strengthen small portions of stippled work it is best to do so with a tracing pencil, either by cross-hatching or by spotting, which will preserve the openness of the work.

It is possible to work over a matt in turpentine colour, first coating the work with oil of tar or spike oil of lavender, and then painting on the shadows and smoothing or graduating with the badger. This, of course, makes a very opaque job even to the extent of closing up or clouding over the fine open scratches left by the scrub, and it ought never to be used with stippled work, as it would destroy its most valuable characteristic.

Mention has already been made of *one-fire* work. The process is a simple one, but calls for particularly smart and unhesitating work. The tracing is done in gum colour, particular attention being paid to having exactly the correct proportion of gum (the quantity of gum in the shading colour should be rather less than that in the tracing colour), and a few of the strongest touches of shadow may be painted in to assist the stipple. When this is thoroughly dry and hard the stipple has to be applied very quickly and unhesitatingly. With the colour in proper condition it ought to be possible to coat on the colour and then stipple it without shifting the tracing lines in the least, though the shaded parts, being thinner, will work up with the stipple, as indeed they ought to. Occasionally some of the finer tracing lines will shift —it may be possible to touch these up afterwards, but if many of them move there is nothing for it but to start afresh. Many expedients have been tried to render the tracing lines hard enough to stand the stippling. Of these the most promising seems to be the use of bichromate of potash or bichromate of ammonium. A small quantity of a 10 per cent. solution of either of these added to the tracing colour ought to render the gum insoluble after an hour's exposure to good daylight (this being the principle on which the carbon and gum bichromate processes in photography are worked), but the result in glass work, owing to the comparatively slight hold which the colour has upon the smooth surface of the glass, is not all that could be wished, and any prolonged stippling will be fatal. Experienced workers are content to rely upon *pure* Gum Arabic and get some wonderful results, even the finest lines in features and hair remaining undisturbed.

The quill point, already mentioned, is very useful on figure work for high lights on hair, drapery, embroidery, jewels, etc. The needle point is sometimes useful in reducing any part of the stipple in which the " smallpox " effect is too marked, and is also of great assistance in very fine matt work for positions close to the eye.

" Spatter " work is occasionally called in to add depth to the shadows in stippled work. The brush required for this is a sash tool or stencil brush cut down till its hairs are only ¼ inch or less in length and perfectly equal. Turpentine colour is perhaps best for the purpose as giving on the whole a finer spray, but gum colour works very well. The brush is rubbed into the colour after the fashion of a stencil brush and is held in the left hand. The forefinger of the right hand is then drawn across the bristles. As they escape from its pressure and spring back to their natural position they throw the colour in tiny spots on to the glass, and a very finely graded effect, similar to a spray, can be got by this means. Here again, of course, there is a risk of piling on the colour too thickly and causing frying in the kiln.

For one-fire work yellow stain may be applied at the same time as the colour, but not to the best advantage. At the high temperature which is required to fuse really good colour stain is much overheated, turns brown, and sometimes disappears altogether. Better results are obtained by giving a second fire for the stain only, at a slightly lower temperature, which will not interfere with the colour and will not run any risk of damaging the surface of the glass. Where considerations of time or economy render it desirable to stain in the colour-fire it must be done by using glass which will stain well at the higher temperature —that is to say, generally speaking, that the greener whites, which are more susceptible to the action of the stain, should be avoided.

Stain is always applied to the *back* of the glass. If it be applied to the same side as the colour the fumes which it gives off in firing will interfere with the fusing of the colour and prevent its becoming fixed.

The application of enamel colours calls for no very special mention. "Flesh colour" is comparatively soft and fires at a slightly lower temperature than tracing colour or shading colour, so that it can always be used in conjunction with them. It is frequently used in front of stain to heighten the effect of gradation by adding an orange brown shade to it, but its principal use is on heads, hands, feet, and other parts of flesh in figure windows. It ought to be sparingly used here on account of its opacity, but generally a very thin film, merely sufficient to kill the greenish tint of the glass and produce a creamy effect, will serve the purpose. A few touches of the needle or the quill on the high lights will greatly assist transparency of effect.

Enamel blue, used for skies and along with stain to produce greens, is much harder, and if brought into contact with unfired tracing colour will cause it to crack and fry. A "soft blue" is also to be had, but it does not produce such a strong colour and is therefore of less value. Purples, crimsons, etc., also require to be kept from contact with tracing colour. A soft black is occasionally used in heraldic work, producing a semi-translucent tone, but the best way of putting in heraldic "sable" is to coat the part solid with tracing colour (gum) and "pick out" a fine diaper with a bone point.

EASELS.

When painting figure work and important ornamental designs made up of a number of small pieces it is necessary to fix them together and hold them up against the light in order to judge the effect of the work as it progresses. This is done by cementing them temporarily to a

Fig. 17.—Design for Leaded Lights,
by Walter J. Pearce.

sheet of clear plate glass with a mixture of beeswax and rosin. The quantities required are, roughly, about four parts of wax to one of rosin, varied according to the season—in summer more rosin will be required than in winter. These are melted together in an iron pannikin, care being taken that the mixture does not catch fire, as it is very apt to do if overheated. The pieces of glass are laid out upon the plate, the cutline drawing being placed below it as a guide. A small quantity of the melted wax mixture is dropped from a small spoon or a palette knife (a short piece of composition gas pipe, cut like a quill pen and fixed on to a wooden handle, makes a good wax-spoon) between the edges of the various pieces so as to cement them firmly to the plate. If too much wax is applied in a very warm and liquid condition it will run between the glass and the easel plate to such an extent as to render the separation of the two a very difficult and risky matter, besides introducing patches of black which will be troublesome during painting. If the wax be too cold it will not run between the pieces and will have no hold. It may be found necessary to re-heat the wax if there be a large surface to work over. The consistency of the wax may be tested by placing a few drops on the plate and chipping it when cold with the point of the palette knife. If it is very tough there is too much wax; if very brittle, too much rosin: in the former case it would hold the glass well but be extremely difficult to remove; in the latter it would break away as soon as the weight of the glass came to bear upon it. As soon as the wax has set, which it does almost immediately, the plate can, with care, be lifted to a vertical position and set upon an easel. Spots of wax which may have dropped upon the surface of the glass must be removed before any colour is applied by chipping them off and then cleaning away all grease with a wet rag; otherwise there will be difficulty in getting the colour to adhere. This cleaning is best done before lifting the plate.

Easels of the ordinary type are, of course, useless for this work, one which will bring no obstacle between the glass and the light being necessary. The required form is illustrated in Fig. 18. These easels are made sometimes about 3 feet or 4 feet high to be set up on the bench, or as large as 6 feet or 7 feet for use upon the floor, the larger patterns occasionally having windlass or screw gear for raising and lowering the plate during the progress of the work. Large plates are generally fixed in wooden frames to give additional strength and facilitate handling. The easel must be

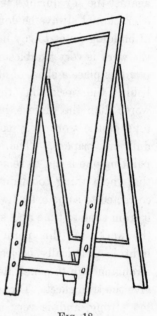

Fig. 18.

set up with its back to the window, and if there be other windows in the room which throw light upon the face of the work it may be necessary to screen them off in order to get the true effect of the painting. The line of white light which occupies the place of the lead between the pieces of glass is very misleading and disconcerting. Experienced workers can ignore it, but it is always best when time permits to paint upon the back of the easel plate black lines to represent the leads. Lamp black mixed with water and a little sugar is suitable for this purpose, being easily applied and easily removed. Whenever possible it is best to be able to see the work clear against the sky during the process of painting. This, however, cannot always be done, and to have a dark background of buildings, etc., to say nothing of window sashes, behind the work is very troublesome. To remedy this some glass painters place a sheet of obscured glass or of tracing paper behind the work; but this remedy is in some respects worse than the disease, inasmuch as it lowers the whole tone of the work very considerably, rendering the effect dull and papery. The consequence of this is that in painting one is apt to remove too much colour and to get the whole thing too thin and weak, though this can be corrected to some extent when using tracing paper by lifting it from time to time and so getting a stronger light upon the work. At this point it may be noted that artificial light is practically useless for glass painting, not being strong enough to penetrate the colour or broad enough to give the true effect. Direct sunlight, on the other hand, is too strong, and is very trying to the eyes. As already stated, a north light is always best.

When painting is finished the plate must be laid upon the bench again, and the removal of the painted glass very carefully undertaken. There is a risk of scratching the painting and of breaking the glass. If the wax be of correct consistency it ought to be possible to dislodge each piece of glass by means of a light, sharp tap in a horizontal direction on the edge of it with the butt of the palette knife, but it may be necessary to chip away the wax with the point of the knife. Large, awkwardly-shaped pieces naturally require more careful handling than the smaller pieces. As each piece of glass is removed all wax is carefully chipped off and returned to the pot for future use. Flat wooden trays are used for carrying the painted glass from the painting room to the kiln. When necessary, one layer of painted glass may be laid over another by placing sheets of paper between to prevent scratching.

It will be evident here that very much depends upon the position which the work is to occupy. If it is to be placed in a building closely surrounded by others it will receive less light, and consequently require to be somewhat less heavily painted than for a more open position with a strong light. The ideal arrangement would be to have the work done *in situ*, but as that is practically impossible, it is advisable to have the fullest information as to position and surroundings in order that allowance may be made for them. Windows placed high up—say in the clerestory of a church—will require greater breadth of treatment than those nearer at hand, and, generally speaking, the principal difference will be that the high lights should be much smaller and the shade tones flatter, while all outlines should naturally be considerably heavier. Far too little attention is paid to these details as a rule, the work being often painted merely with an eye to its appearance on the easel, without regard to its ultimate position.

SPRAY PAINTING.

The Aerograph and other similar devices for spray painting can be turned to very good account in glass work, not

only on account of their speed in working, but also because
of their avoidance of some of the technical difficulties
inseparable from the usual process. In the eyes of those
who are sticklers for precedent and tradition and who wish
to preserve the time-honoured characteristics of the craft
they must, of course, be eternally taboo. On the other
hand, to workers who look upon the end as justifying the
means there will be apparent both artistic and economic
reasons for their employment.

These machines consist of two main parts—an air compressor, by means of which a steady air pressure is main-
tained, and, connected to it by means of a flexible tube of
rubber or metal, a hand-piece which comprises the jet
from which the spray of colour is projected, valves controlling the air supply and the flow of colour, and the cup
in which the supply of colour is carried. The valves are
operated by pressure of the fingers upon a spring trigger,
and the hand-piece is easily operated by one hand, leaving
the other free to hold the work or to steady its neighbour
by means of a mahl-stick or otherwise. Different sizes of
instruments will be found necessary for differing work. A
fairly large instrument held about a foot distant from the
glass to be operated upon will produce a coat of colour in
character something between a matt and a stipple, which
can be worked upon with the scrubs in the usual way, but
is too fine to allow of the use of the finger tips as upon
stipple. Or with a smaller "brush" at a shorter range
shadows can be applied just where they are required, painting them on with a softness of gradation which cannot be
attained by any other means, either over a stipple with the
object of merely strengthening the shadows, or without

the assistance of the stipple to produce the full effect. In either case considerable practice is required to overcome the difficulties of handling the instrument and of controlling the spray, regulating the air supply and the colour supply. Tracing or shading colour ground in gum and water gives very good results. It must have a larger proportion of water than when used with pencils, but it is quite an easy matter to make it too thin. Too much water will make the colour run when the glass is upright on the easel. The colour must also be ground very fine—coarse colour tends to choke the jet and make the delivery of the spray very unequal, besides producing a gritty effect on the glass.

In handling the instrument it will be found that the first pressure upon the trigger opens the air supply, while the pressure has to be increased to open the colour valve. The result is that the colour valve is apt to open somewhat suddenly and unexpectedly, and a very delicate control of the trigger is required to keep the supply of colour constant. This can be assisted to some degree by altering the relation of the colour supply to the air supply, which can be done by means of a regulating screw, so as to give a greater or less supply of colour. Cloudiness is the most frequent fault in large surfaces treated by the spray method, and this can only be guarded against by careful regulation of the valves and a delicate control of the trigger, though in some circumstances, and under intelligent control, it might be accepted as a welcome improvement on the flat matt.

Considered from an artistic and technical point of view, sprayed shadows must appear lacking in character when compared with the brush work of the scrub, which is much more capable of expressing the individuality of the worker. As a means of covering a large surface the air-brush is certainly more rapid, when a little experience has been gained, than the flat brush and badger or stippler, and when it is thus used in conjunction with the scrub there can be no artistic objection to the result. Piling on the colour too thickly has to be guarded against for fear of frying in the kiln, but there is, on the whole, rather less risk of this with the spray than with the ordinary processes. It will be found that a spray, like a badger matt, seems to lose more density in firing than a stipple does.

For outline work the spray does not appear to be at all suitable: though the smaller instruments can be made to produce a line of a kind, it has always a soft cloudy edge, which gives it a very weak effect as compared with the strength and firm edges of the lead line. Its sphere of usefulness in glass work must be confined to shading, the outlining being done as of old with the tracing pencil.

The outfit is rather expensive and would not pay for itself except where there is constant employment for it. In addition to two or more hand-pieces, an air compressor is required—the necessary working pressure being not less than 30 lbs. to the square inch. Small compressors, with metal reservoirs, operated by the foot are to be had, but are fatiguing and somewhat distracting in use. Larger machines, capable of working two or more hand-pieces at the same time, can be had, but require to be driven by a small gas engine or other mechanical power. In addition to the " Aerograph " there are other makes at varying prices on the market with distinctive features of their own. In purchasing a hand-piece it is essential to observe that

the air valve closes tight, so that there may be no leakage
of pressure when the instrument is temporarily put out of
action. Accessibility for cleaning is also very important,
especially where so heavy a material as glass colour has to
be used. Jets and valves become choked through the colour
drying in them or through grit and other foreign substances
in the colour sticking in them. It should therefore be
possible to take the whole thing to pieces for cleaning.
Convenience and ease in handling have to be considered—
in the case of continuous work some patterns are apt to
cramp the hand through having too large or too small a
grip, while too strong a trigger spring is likely to have the
same effect.

Rough Cast Plate.

Rough cast plate, painted and stained, does not receive
quite so much attention nowadays as it merits. Having no
restrictions in the shape of lead lines, very great freedom of
design is possible. It is, of course, non-transparent, but
just on that account it is specially useful for ceiling lights,
corridor windows, door panels, etc., where light without
view is required, and it can be bent for cupolas. It has one
great advantage over leaded lights in that it is unquestion-
ably weatherproof, whereas with lead lights, when bent to
cupola form, it is generally considered advisable to give
them an outer protection of rough cast. It is generally
decorated only with Renaissance arabesques in outline and
stain, but there are possibilities of very much greater
variety in treatment. Coloured enamels, blue, crimson,
etc., can be used on it with perfect freedom, as it has no
transparency for them to destroy, and well-designed patches
of black have a surprising value. Ornament of a Moresque

character lends itself fairly well to such treatment, but generally a very considerable portion of the ground must be kept clear of ornament to pass a sufficient amount of light.

This material has been almost entirely neglected by up-to-date designers, which is rather a pity, as it gives such good opportunity for free conventional designs based on plant forms, for the colour of which enamels would be very satisfactory. Plates of very large size can be fired in bending kilns, and the heat required to bend the glass is quite sufficient to fuse even the hardest colours.

FLASHED GLASS AND ACID.

Flashed glass affords a most valuable aid to the glass painter in the possibility it gives by the use of acid of obtaining two colours on one piece of glass in a perfectly legitimate way and in keeping with the best traditions of the craft. It may be used to avoid a piece of intricate leading or weak construction, or to produce diaper patterns, say in yellow on ruby or blue, or *vice versâ*. It is useful in heraldic work when details of blazonry become too small to look well in lead work (flashed ruby and blue do not quite accurately represent the heraldic gules and azure, but the difference is comparatively small), and it can be used to introduce a yellow centre into a red flower. Acid is also used occasionally to modify the colour of a piece of ruby or blue glass, giving a certain amount of variation from light to dark, but should be used in such a case only as a last resource. It requires very great care to produce even a passable effect of shading, and it can never compare with the natural gradation of a good piece of antique glass. There may be a necessity here for a warning against any attempt to impart interest to flashed sheet glass in this way. The attempt is occasionally made, and the result is always blank failure. The glass is always poor and thin by comparison with antique, and any attempt at "faking" seems to make it look poorer still.

The removal or modification of the flashed colour is effected by means of hydrofluoric acid, which has the power of dissolving glass. For the method of using the acid the reader is referred to Chapter IV. It should be noted here that flashed glass is generally cut on the "clear" side, as the diamond does not cut properly on the flash side, but when it is wanted for treatment with acid it is well to reverse the drawing when cutting so as to be able to paint on the flashed side. This will prevent the traced outline seeming to be detached from the colour, as it might seem to be when seen at an angle if the flash were on the outside.

KILNS

Kilns for firing painted glass vary a good deal in construction and system of working. Descriptions of three principal types will perhaps be sufficient. The old-fashioned muffle kiln, fired with coal or coke, is illustrated in Fig. 19. The muffle (A) is a strong box of cast iron, say 24 inches by 18 inches by 18 inches, with slides (B) on the inside to carry a number of wrought iron plates from $\frac{1}{4}$ inch to $\frac{3}{8}$ inch thick. It is closed in front with a door (C) of cast iron having a cone-shaped spy-hole (D) and held in position by a bar of wrought iron (E) dropping into notches (F). It is built into a firebrick furnace, having flues (G) spaced all around it. The front is closed in with a door of firebrick in two parts (H). The iron plates are covered with finely powdered whiting sprinkled on through a sieve, and the pieces of glass to be fired are laid carefully upon this, care being taken not to disturb the whiting. The glass ought not to come within half an inch or an inch of the edge of the plate, and the pieces must not be allowed to overlap or touch each other, as in that case they would

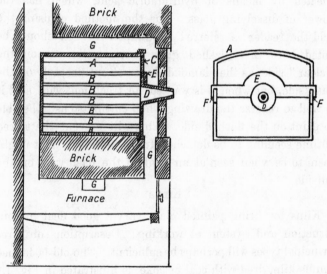

FIG. 19.

probably stick together. Every precaution must be taken to have both kiln and whiting perfectly free from damp (which would raise steam and damage the painting), even to the extent of heating up the kiln and whiting before putting in the glass. The plates with the glass having been placed in the kiln, the iron door is placed in position and the interstices carefully closed with a plaster of stucco and water applied with a trowel. The space between this iron door and the firebrick door forms one of the flues, and the smoke must be prevented from entering the muffle. The firebrick door is then closed and plastered up in the same way, and the fire started.

A kiln of the size stated will take from four to six hours to fire, much depending on arrangement of flues, strength of draught, etc. Arrangement of flues has also a great deal to do with equal heating, which is most important, and in many new kilns of this type the position of flues may have to be altered after trial in order to get the best results. The progress of heating can be watched after the first hour or so by means of the spy-hole, which is provided for that purpose, the interior of the muffle becoming incandescent as it heats up. The spy-hole generally commands a view, more or less complete, of at least two plates, and as the iron becomes red-hot the glass can be seen as a number of black patches lying upon it. Precautions must be taken to ensure as equal heating as possible. This may be affected to a considerable extent even when there are no dampers to the several flues by keeping the fire to the back or the front of the furnace. Occasionally the furnace is made with a door at the back of the kiln as well as in front. Gradually the glass heats up and finally becomes practically invisible. The colour on its surface is last to feel the heat and remains for some time matt and dull. When it becomes glossy firing is complete. Allowance has to be made for the fact that the great mass of iron and brick will hold the heat for a long time, and so it may be found necessary to draw the fire before the colour has properly fluxed. To allow the glass to become overheated is disastrous. The softer glasses, such as some of the antiques—green, for instance—reach a semi-liquid condition in which they begin to flow. The grain of the sifted whiting is impressed upon the lower side, the clean-cut edges become rounded, and in extreme cases pieces may even lose their shape. In addition to that, the colour, which inevitably loses some of its density, may be so much reduced as to render re-painting necessary. The brilliance and transparency of all glasses, but especially the softer ones, are affected by repeated firing, and so it ought to be avoided. Moreover, in repeated painting the technique, texture, and quality of brushwork become lost as one working is put over another, and the work never has the freshness and distinction nor the translucent sparkle of work which is finished in one fire.

The kiln will require at least as long to cool as it takes to fire, and the cooling must on no account be hurried because of the risk of breaking the glass by too sudden a change of temperature. No door should be opened until it is possible to handle it without injury to the skin, though occasionally this rule is evaded by the use of leather gloves or grips. Even after the iron door has been removed the plates should remain in the muffle for some time, and at this stage the glass must be very carefully guarded from draughts. It is not safe to remove a piece of glass from the plate until it can be done with the naked fingers.

Gas kilns divide themselves into two main types—the carriage or closed kiln, and the open or continuous firing kiln. In gas kilns the time required for firing is considerably less, but this is counterbalanced by their smaller capacity. This, however, has its advantage when small quantities of glass have to be dealt with. One small piece would require as much coal to fire it in a muffle kiln as a kilnful.

In the carriage type of gas kiln (Fig. 20) there is only one plate (A) mounted on a carriage (B) which runs upon iron rails under a firebrick arch (C) and closed in by iron

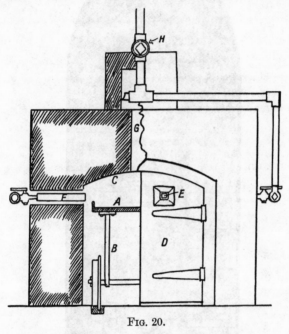

Fig. 20.

doors (D) having a spy-hole in each (E). The gas-burners are placed at the spring of the arch on either side (F) and allow the gas flames to play upon the soffit of the arch, the products of combustion escaping by a row of central flues at G. The main stop-cock is at H, but each of the burners has a separate tap by which it can be regulated in case of necessity.

FIG. 21.—Design for Memorial Window,
by Wm. Aikman.

The glass in a carriage kiln is generally laid upon a bed of whiting $\frac{1}{2}$ inch to 1 inch deep, the burners are lighted up, the carriage run in, and the doors closed. (At this point it should be noted that considerable care is necessary in lighting the gas. If any considerable time is allowed to elapse between turning on the gas and applying the flame, the escaping gas will mix with the air in the confined space and cause great risk of explosion. This applies to all gas kilns. The light must be applied almost immediately after turning on the gas.) Any opening between the bottom of the doors and the brick flooring should be closed by piling dry whiting against it to prevent the ingress of cold air. All the air required by the burners, which are, of course, of the Bunsen type, burning a mixture of gas and air, passes through the openings at the sides in which the burners are placed. It is necessary to begin firing with a low pressure of gas, increasing the pressure gradually so as not to heat up the glass too quickly. Firing will take from one to two hours. There being no muffle between the glass and the gas flames, the glass is visible through the spy-hole during the whole operation of firing, and progress is perhaps a little more difficult to judge. There is, however, no mistaking the change in colour from the cold blue flame of the gas in the cold kiln to the red glow which must be reached in order to flux the colour, and the gradual glazing of the colour is rather more easily seen owing to the presence of the gas flames. The kiln, having been so quickly heated up, will cool equally quickly, and the colour will not have the prolonged " stewing " which it receives in a muffle. Therefore the glazing of the colour must be carried farther, and in fact completed, before turning off the gas. The same precautions with regard to cooling off must be observed before removing the glass from the kiln. The plate in a kiln of this description may measure as large as 4 feet by 3 feet, and is therefore capable of firing sheets of glass nearly approaching that size, but it is advisable to leave a

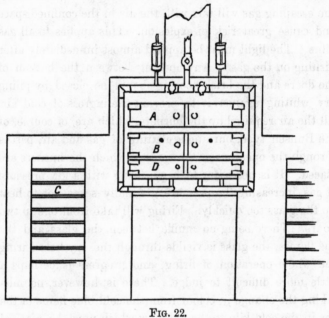

FIG. 22.

margin of three or four inches between the glass and the edge of the plate whenever possible. This kiln can also be used for bending in sizes up to 3 feet by 2 feet.

The open or continuous firing kiln uses plates of 24 inches by 18 inches and has two heating chambers, one above the other, the upper (A) for "heating up," the lower (B) for "finishing" (Fig. 22). The plates in this case, of which there

may be two dozen or more to one kiln, are made of cast iron,
and have an upturned edging all round to give additional
strength and to prevent any chance of the glass slipping off
in handling.   These plates have to be lifted into and out of
the kiln while hot with a huge toasting fork which is
provided for the purpose.   The plate is only sifted over
with whiting as the weight must be kept down to facilitate
lifting. On either side of the kiln proper are two "temperate"
chambers (C) used for heating and cooling off.   In using
this kiln the burners, which are enclosed by the door (D), are
first lighted with a low pressure to warm up the whole
concern and drive off damp, and a surprising amount of condensation will sometimes appear on the iron doors, etc.
This, of course, applies to all kilns when they are allowed
to become thoroughly cold.   A plate, ready sprinkled with
whiting, is placed in each chamber.   As soon as the one in
the lower chamber, immediately above the burners, becomes
hot enough to be uncomfortable to the touch, it is removed
by slipping the fork under it and lifting it to an adjacent
bench.   The glass is placed upon it, and it is returned to
the lower chamber.   The plate in the upper chamber is
now brought out, filled with glass, and returned to its place.
It is best when beginning work with a cold kiln to heat up
as many plates as will be required.   They can then be
filled with glass and placed in the temperate chamber to
await their turn.

The progress of firing is watched as usual through the
spy-holes and must be carried to completion, as cooling is
very rapid with this kiln.   When it is complete the red-hot
plate has to be lifted from the finishing chamber and
placed in one of the temperate chambers to cool off.   The

operation has to be smartly performed, and it will be evident that it is absolutely necessary to have the kiln-room quite free from draughts, as a puff of cold air upon the hot plate might break every piece of glass. The awkwardness of lifting caused by the weight of the plate and its leverage on the fork is now increased by the heat, which prevents the hand being placed so near the plate as before, but this can be guarded against to some extent by using a leather glove or a wrapping of sackcloth on the hand. The doors of the finishing chamber are opened, the plate smartly lifted out and placed on the top shelf of one of the temperate chambers, where it will get most benefit from the heat of the kiln. The plate in the top chamber is moved down to the lower one, and a fresh plate with glass which has been waiting in the " temperate " chamber takes its place. So the operation can be repeated until the whole twenty-four plates have been through the kiln. The longer the kiln is in operation the more quickly will the glass heat up, and the more slowly will it cool. The risk of breakage during cooling is, of course, less after two or three hours, but it is no uncommon thing for pieces to " fly " in the temperate chamber when the kiln is newly started. This can be guarded against by giving the whole kiln a good heating before putting in any glass at all. In this kiln two gauges are fitted on the gas supply pipe in order that the pressure on both sides may be kept exactly equal.

Considerable opposition was made to the use of gas kilns when they were first introduced. It was argued that the gas fumes would injure the colour, and that the long, slow heating in the muffle must be more effective in fluxing the colour than the short, fierce firing of the gas kiln. These arguments seem, however, to have lost any weight they may have had, and at the present time the gas kiln has practically superseded the muffle. Any smoking or firing back of the burners in a gas kiln will, of course, at once cause trouble, the presence of smoke preventing the colour from fluxing.

A very effective kiln for small work can be made with an ordinary kitchen oven for the muffle, a special door with spy-hole being made for it of cast iron. The thin metal allows of fairly rapid firing, but there is more risk of unequal heating, and it will, of course, wear out quicker than one of heavier section.

Small pieces of glass can be successfully fired in the small gas muffles used for enamelling upon metals. When the quantity of work turned out does not warrant the expense of fitting up a kiln, glass can be sent to one of the firms who make a business of firing glass for all comers. There are two or three of these in London, who can be trusted to do the work intelligently, giving every attention as to correct temperature, etc. Their charge is generally about sixpence per square foot.

DESIGN.

The majority of what has already been said regarding design for leaded lights will apply equally to design for stained glass. The lead line must be looked upon as one of the essential points : it is the means of introducing colour—the means of construction. The painting is really a secondary affair, introduced merely to help out and complete the work which has been more than half done by the lead and the glass. There are, of course, exceptions to this rule. The lead lines may be simple squares or quarries to which the main ornamental interest remains to be added by paint and stain, as in the case of Renaissance arabesques, but it is useless for the painted design to attempt to ignore or stultify the lead work, which is much too strong to be set aside. Desperate attempts are occasionally made to modify the lead work so that it shall not interfere with certain features of painted ornament, with the result that the cutting is rendered needlessly difficult, the risk of breakage increased, and the appearance of the work when seen with a face-light upon it becomes much more uninteresting than it need be. Efforts are sometimes made in many more or less ingenious ways to conceal the existence of the lead, which is a mistake from every point of view. The lead line must be frankly accepted, given its proper, rightful place in the importance of things, and the painted work so co-related with it that the two shall be thoroughly harmonious and mutually helpful. There seems to be a feeling sometimes that the lead line is heavy and clumsy and that the thinner line possible with painted work is more desirable, and yet the lead line will be introduced in a reluctant, blundering fashion for the sake of introducing colour. We have all seen the swag on which a great bunch of leaded ruby and green fruit and foliage hangs by pitiful little stained ribbons from a still more pitiful spray of stained ornament. It is only too obvious that there is no relation between the two and that no attempt has been made to bring them into harmony. Such heavy masses of lead and colour ought to be led up to and supported by other features of proportionate importance, either leaded or painted with a good firm line.

It should never be forgotten that light is constantly being refracted in its passage through the air—that after passing through the window it continues to spread. The result of this spreading is that dark lines, whether of lead or paint, appear narrower than they really are, and patches of dark colour appear much smaller than equal-sized patches of white or light tints. So you will find that the $\frac{1}{4}$-inch lead which appears so wide and clumsy when held in the hand becomes comparatively unobtrusive when in its place in the window, while the painted line which you thought about the right strength practically vanishes. By comparison the narrow line will appear to lose more than the wide. This has to be allowed for in the design, and the farther the window is to be placed from the eye the greater must be the allowance. This difficulty comes to a climax in church window work, where in a window placed high above the floor the form and expression of a face will seem to alter with every passing cloud, appearing thin, severe, and ascetic when the light is dull, and almost fat and jolly under a burst of sunshine.

Colour is also affected, though to a less degree, by the same fact. Light colours lose force and become almost washy, while dark colours are in danger of becoming black spots. Careful balance of colour, therefore, is absolutely necessary, and this is one of the strongest reasons why the designer ought to give personal attention to the selection of the glass, instead of leaving it, as is so often done, entirely to the glass cutter.

With regard to style of ornament, there never can be anything more suited to stained glass than the work which was done in the thirteenth and fourteenth centuries in

France and England. The fifteenth century saw the beginning of the falling off, when the relation between leaded and painted work was destroyed, and the painting exploited at the expense of the leading. So the most suitable style of design will be of such a character as will recall the colour glories of that period. There must, of course, be occasions when a large proportion of white glass will be necessary—when the illuminating power of the window is specially required or when harmony with a light scheme of decoration is necessary. For such circumstances we can seek suggestion in the early work of the fifteenth century, before the glazier's work had been seriously eclipsed by that of the painter. This, of course, does not mean that all glass design should be Gothic. That cannot be. But in our balancing of colour and our co-relation of leading and painting we ought to try to conform to the mediæval standard. To copy the design of the period serves no good purpose—we cannot by that means ensure a successful result—but by recognising the limitations and the possibilities of the material as they were recognised by the mediæval designer we can design something which will be in keeping with the spirit and feeling of our own times, will afford us an opportunity of showing our own individuality, and stand a chance of favourable comparison with the old work. At the present time the majority of what may be called "commercial" ecclesiastical stained glass is a heartless copy of fifteenth century work. It varies, of course, in detail, and in the treatment of the figure portion frequently accords very well with the practice of earlier and better periods, but for its ornamental portion it almost invariably relies on perpendicular canopy work. As far as

balance of colour goes there is no objection to this. The
mass of white or light tinted glass contrasts well with the
stronger colour in the figure portion and serves a useful
and laudable purpose in transmitting light for the illumina-
tion of the building. But why copy in glass (a transparent
or at least translucent material) the shafts and pinnacles,
crockets and finials, of wood and stone work ? A sculptured
figure, coloured or uncoloured, in a sculptured niche may
be a very fine thing in its way ; but is either the figure or
the niche such a very desirable thing as to warrant our
copying it in a totally different material ? Why not seek
inspiration elsewhere, say from nature, and place our
figures beneath a canopy of ornament more or less con-
ventionalised from one or other of the many beautiful
forms of the vegetable kingdom, many of which are pecu-
liarly fitted for the purpose because of the symbolism which
has been associated with them ?

There is too much copying of styles and periods nowadays. There is no reason why we should set ourselves
down to copy the craftsman of the fifteenth century—he did
not copy his predecessors of the tenth. If he had done, we
would certainly have seen less good in his work to copy.
And yet how many of us sit down to copy Renaissance
which was copied from Roman which was copied from
Greek ! And the Greek work grew naturally out of
its surroundings in the sunny South—how is it going to
suit our surroundings in a different climate after the lapse
of centuries ? Our laws, our habits and customs, our
costumes, we modify to meet the requirements of our times
and circumstances ; why may not our art also grow with
us ? We have developed our music—fancy going to the

Opéra to hear Gregorian chants—why may we not have twentieth century design ?

At the present time, as has already been mentioned, painted glass has been to some extent ousted from public favour by leaded lights, partly on account of the comparative cheapness of the latter, but also because of their being more translucent than a great deal of painted work. Here there is a useful suggestion to guide us in design for painted glass. While making as full use as possible of the opportunities which the pigment gives us of adding the interest of detail to lead work and colour, we must avoid putting on "shading" to such an extent as to destroy translucency, or so covering up a light background with ornament as to produce a heavy effect. Shading, whether on figure or ornament, must not be of a realistic character or attempt to convey an impression of relief. In addition to the usual conditions of decorative work on an opaque surface we have here the added difficulty of working on a translucent surface—the light by which we see the design must pass through the material. So any excess of shadow will stop the light and destroy the character of the window, both useful and ornamental. Variation of colour, then, should be sought for as much as possible in the glass itself, which in spite of gradation of tone still preserves translucency, and pigment shading, which makes for opacity, kept within the smallest possible limits.

The ideal window would be one in which the whole effect was obtained by the use of lead and glass only—a leaded light—but in figure and other elaborate work the lead outline will not give us the delicate definition we require, and the glass, no matter how beautifully variegated or streaked, will not give its variations of tone exactly where we want them. So we have to use the paint, but *only* as an aid to the lead and the glass.

The use of silver stain also is worthy of a little more consideration than it sometimes receives. It is one of the most characteristic, and therefore, from an artistic point of view, one of the most valuable, features of the process. Too little use is generally made of the great range of variation, from palest lemon to deepest orange, of which it is capable, and it appears, as a rule, merely as a brassy yellow of annoyingly mechanical monotony.

The employment of enamel colours in glass painting must remain a question for individual taste. In ecclesiastical work there is not much call for them, except, perhaps, in modification of flesh tones ; in domestic work they can be made very useful in modification of stain, but it is advisable to confine their use to small spots, where their opacity will be less of a blot upon the translucency of the whole window than if they were applied to larger surfaces. This matter has, however, already been touched upon when dealing with pigments, and it is unnecessary to say more of it here.

Amongst the more general considerations governing design for church windows may be mentioned the following :—Position, whether high above the floor or more on a level with the eye—whether in an aisle or chapel, where it can only be viewed from a short distance or at the end of nave or transept with a long vista—whether placed clear against open sky or overshadowed by buildings. All these must affect not only the scale of the work, but the colour scheme. One important point with regard to church

window design is this : that when seen from a distance at
which it is impossible to recognise figures or subjects the
masses of colour should be pleasing in outline and harmonious in their relation to one another. It is possible for
masses of colour to assume most grotesque shapes and
appearances when it is not possible to see all the details.
Relation to other windows and scheme of decoration—this
does not necessarily mean that the new work should conform absolutely in detail of ornament or in arrangement of
subject and ornament with that around it, but the fact that
it is only a unit in the architectural scheme must be
remembered. Just as the carving on the capitals of the
nave arcading may be varied in motif and treatment,
while all conveying one impression of scale and richness, so
the windows may be varied in detail, but should convey a
similar impression as regards scale and colour. Colour is
perhaps most important in this connection, and it is often
the most difficult to cope with. Where a designer finds
that his work has to be placed alongside of windows in
which the colour, as is too often the case, is hopelessly
crude, he must endeavour to work to a similar *strength* of
tone, while keeping his colours more harmonious. A
difficult point with regard to relation to other windows is
that a window may be placed in such a position, say at
right angles or opposite to others, as to have its light and
colour very seriously affected by the light passing through
them. Generally speaking, windows which have the sun
falling directly upon them should be dealt with first in any
continuous scheme. It frequently happens that the east
window, being the most important, is first filled with
coloured glass, without sufficient consideration being given

Fig. 23.—Memorial Window.
From the Studios of Wm. Pape, Leeds.

to its position, and that the light passing through the windows on the south side of the chancel will fall upon the face of it and entirely destroy its effect. To deal first with these side windows, which are comparatively seldom seen, does not recommend itself as a good way out of the difficulty. A solution has been attempted in many cases by coating the side windows with paint to tone down the strength of the light or fitting blinds, which must look more or less incongruous. A more sensible alternative is to treat the east window in as light a scheme of colour as possible, using plenty of white and light tints, and keeping the colour confined to backgrounds and carefully considered small patches well distributed over the window.

CHAPTER IV

EMBOSSED GLASS

EMBOSSING has generally been looked upon as one of the
least artistic of glass processes, but its favour amongst the
majority of people would seem to have been none the less
on that account. In fact, while its popularity has fluc-
tuated to a very great extent, it has never been seriously
challenged by any other process. Enamelling and sand-
blast, the two processes most like to it in their results, hold
some sway in certain circumstances, but have not the same
variety of application, partly owing to the details in which
they differ from embossed work. The many good points of
the embossing process seem likely to ensure a continuation
of its popularity in spite of all the new rivals which appear
against it, and the gradual modification and development
of the process seem to add to these good points year by
year. It has been used at various times in combination
with other processes, such as gilding, oil painting, glass
staining, mirror silvering, etc., and in every case it has
added its full quota of interest and value to the work. The
latest combination into which it has been introduced is that
with Brilliant Cutting, and it is perhaps the most successful
of all, the qualities of the two processes, or rather of the
results produced by them, being quite of a complementary
character. The combination of brilliant cutting with two-
or three-acid work produces the most artistic and ornate

effect which has yet been attained by these processes, and where the design is good and practical goes a long way to absolve the work from the charge of being inartistic. Unfortunately, however, good design both in Embossed and Brilliant Cut work is somewhat rare. In fâct, generally speaking, the more elaborate the work and the finer the tone effect, the worse is the design. There is, of course, absolutely no reason why this should be so, and fortunately there has been a very great improvement in this respect within the last few years. The work now being turned out by a few of the more advanced workers can lay claim to both originality and excellence of design, while still showing to the full the fine tone effects which the process is capable of producing.

ACIDS.

The process owes its existence to the power possessed by hydrofluoric acid of dissolving glass, and can be modified in various ways by diluting or mixing the acid to produce different results. The fluorine gas which is held in solution, and which very readily escapes from the liquid in the shape of its characteristic "fumes," produces a frosted surface on any glass which it comes into contact with, and the acid has been used in this way—exposing the glass only to the fumes—but not to any great extent of recent years. The liquid, while dissolving away the surface, has the contrary effect of leaving it comparatively clear, but when modified, or neutralised, by the addition of an alkali, produces a dense white frosted surface. This combination of acid and alkali goes by the name of White Acid, and forms the principal agent in the compound process which is known to glass-workers as French, or Triple, Embossing.

Hydrofluoric acid is produced by heating fluor spar (calcium fluoride) in concentrated sulphuric acid in a retort made of lead and condensing the resultant gas in water, and formerly had to be prepared by glass-workers themselves, but can now be obtained ready for use from manufacturers, such as Messrs. Wilkinson & Son, Attercliffe, Sheffield, and Messrs. Cruikshanks, Birmingham.

White acid can also be obtained ready made, but, as no special apparatus is required, most workers prefer to prepare their own to suit the particular style of work which they have in hand. This course is, in fact, advisable, as white acid is very apt to go wrong and may require frequent "doctoring" to keep it in working order. Although popularly known as white "acid," this mixture is not really acid in its nature—when in proper working order a test with litmus paper shows it to be distinctly alkaline. Red litmus paper dipped into it turns blue, while blue litmus paper dipped into fluoric acid of course changes to red.

One of the most satisfactory recipes for the production of white acid is as follows:—

Fluoric Acid (full strength)	...	...	...	$\frac{1}{2}$ pint.
Carbonate of Soda	...	...	...	$1\frac{1}{2}$ lbs.
Water ...	...	...	...	...	1 pint.

The soda (common washing soda) must be selected, only clear crystals being used and the white powder discarded. The crystals may be crushed to accelerate solution. The above quantities may have to be modified under certain conditions, weather, for instance, having a considerable effect upon the mixture, and only an actual test upon a sample piece of glass can be taken as an indication that

the mixture is in working order. It ought to produce a
dense white obscure in about an hour.

Another recipe substitutes carbonate of ammonia for carbonate of soda, adding the carbonate to a mixture of acid
and water a small lump at a time till effervescence ceases.
This mixture works perfectly well, but does not produce
such a dense white as the first. Its fullest effect is reached
in about twenty-five minutes.

A third recipe—Soda Ash, 1 lb., Rain Water, $\frac{1}{2}$ gallon,
Fluoric Acid, $\frac{1}{2}$ lb.—also produces a very weak effect.

UTENSILS.

The only materials proof against the action of fluoric
acid are lead, gutta-percha, india-rubber, pitch and other
resinous substances, and greases. It is stored in bottles of
gutta-percha, or occasionally of lead, the former being
generally used because of its light weight. The gutta-
percha is somewhat expensive, but if carefully handled is
practically everlasting. Troughs to hold the acid when
small pieces of glass have to be immersed in it are made of
wood lined with lead, sometimes of wood coated with
beeswax, tallow, or other resin or grease, and even
in emergency of pieces of glass coated and stuck
together with beeswax. When acid is used upon a large
plate of glass the trough is dispensed with and the edge of
the plate surrounded by a "dyke" or "wall" composed of
tallow—pure or mixed with other substance—or mixtures
such as asphaltum and beeswax. This wall is also used to
cut off large surfaces which the acid is not required to
touch, so reducing the quantity of acid needed for the
operation. Owing to the constant escape of the fluorine

gas, the acid loses strength whenever it is exposed to the air, and so it is necessary to use always as small a quantity as possible and to keep the bottles well stoppered. The stock bottle ought to have its stopper sealed down with a plentiful coat of tallow. The fumes escape from full-strength acid so profusely as to be quite visible like a yellow smoke, and are not only obnoxious, but dangerous. Even at a moderate working strength they will cause bleeding of the throat and nostrils in persons in whom these organs happen to be weak, while they commonly cause severe smarting of the eyes, which is only relieved by a flow of tears. On the other hand, they are said to have a beneficial effect in cases of pulmonary consumption—a disease which is practically non-existent among people who handle this acid. On account of these fumes the acid cannot be stored anywhere in proximity to a stock of glass without risk of obscuring the surface of the glass. Acid work, wherever possible, is done in a separate room or building with special provision for ventilation in order to carry off the gas. The fumes from white acid are not nearly so strong or so troublesome to the workers.

Acid is most frequently used on plate glass—sheet glass is occasionally used as a cheap substitute. Flashed sheet glass—generally ruby and blue—is frequently used both for decorative and advertising purposes. Flashed antique glass, for various reasons, does not lend itself to this purpose so readily as does sheet glass—for instance, it is made in smaller sizes and is much more expensive.

In ordinary embossed plate work the design is etched into the surface of the glass by means of the acid to a depth of perhaps one-thirtieth of an inch. The pattern then appears slightly depressed with a surface very slightly roughened and, by comparison with the clear plate, obscure. The surface is then ground with flour emery until it becomes obscure, the design being protected from the action of the emery by the fact of its lying beneath the surface. When the " bite " is shallow, there is, of course, considerable risk that the grinding, especially if prolonged, will obliterate the pattern. Parts of the design—generally large background spaces—which have to be kept clear are surrounded by a broad etched line (not less than half an inch) to prevent encroachment of the grinder.

In French embossing the process is much more compli-cated. The design is made up of a series of graduated tones as follows :—

1. White Acid.

2. White Acid reduced one degree with hydrofluoric acid.

3. White Acid reduced two degrees with hydrofluoric acid.

4. White Acid reduced three degrees with hydrofluoric acid.

5. Clear Plate.

6. Brilliant Cut (not always used).

The grinding is in this case dispensed with altogether. The tones begin with the white obscure produced by the white acid. This is then cleared by the application of hydrofluoric, the tone being regulated by the length of time during which the acid is allowed to act, varying from about five minutes for No. 2 tone to half an hour for No. 4. So by varying the length of time three or four different tones may be obtained, coming back almost, but not quite, to the clear plate, with the Brilliant Cut as a supreme effect. In actual practice the brilliant cutting is done first. Then it and all parts which are to remain clear are protected by Brunswick black, and the white acid is applied over the whole remaining surface of the plate. More black is then added to protect all parts of the design on which the full strength of the white acid is required, and the plate is subjected to the action of hydrofluoric acid to obtain the first degree of reduction. Another addition of black is followed by the second reduction, and so on. A very delicate and elaborate design, of a "lacey" character, is thus obtainable, which is occasionally enhanced by the addition of Gilding or Silver Stain. In Flashed glass work the coloured film is entirely removed from the surface of the glass where not required, and the glass is then backed, as, for instance, in the case of lamp panes and illuminated signs, with opal glass, figured rolled, muffled, etc. The crude colours of flashed ruby and blue sheet glass constitute a very valid objection to their use in many cases, and where a more delicate effect is required it can be obtained by using flashed opal glass, backing this, if necessary, with pale tints of Rolled Cathedral or Muffled. Here again the flat chalky appearance of the opal may be objectionable, but another alternative offers itself in the shape of Reamy Opalescent sheet, in which the white is not nearly so dense and is shaded in a very pleasing manner. For lettering in leaded lights for doors of hotels and other business premises this glass produces probably the most artistic effect which is procurable, being readily legible without being loud and obtrusive. A sheet opal glass, flashed with quiet flat colours, such as turquoise, yellow, orange, and ruby, is made in France and gives nice quiet effects for lettering, but is not always reliable under acid, being rather apt to

corrode.   Flashed sheet blue is also very liable to corrosion.
The only safeguards against this trouble, which entirely
spoils the appearance of the work, are to avoid the use of
over-strong acid, and to keep wiping away, with a " spud "
or mop made of a lump of cotton wool on the end of a stick,
the scum formed as the flash dissolves in the acid.   Ruby
produces much less scum and is less liable to corrosion, but
in the case of a thick flash and prolonged exposure to the
acid the use of the mop is advisable.

It has already been pointed out that utensils used for
acid should be made of gutta-percha.   In addition to bottles,
of which several are necessary for various strengths of acid,
one or two funnels will be required, jugs for measuring,
and a bucket with a close-fitting lid.   The bucket will be
required for mixing acid with water, and for catching the
acid when poured off a plate.   It will also be found useful
for flooding a plate with acid, because, especially if it be
made with a lip as it ought to be, it pours so much more
steadily than a bottle, the bubbling of which is very apt
to splash the acid over the low wall surrounding the plate.
The lid will be found useful for covering the bucket when
acid is allowed to remain in it for short periods instead of
returning it to the bottle.   India-rubber stoppers for the
bottles are generally most satisfactory.   Gutta-percha is
rather hard and cannot be depended upon to fit closely
enough.   Wood well coated with grease or oil will serve
—cork is quite useless.

RESISTS.

The most commonly used " resist " for hydrofluoric acid
is Brunswick black, but the ordinary variety obtained in

most oil shops is not to be depended upon. It can be obtained, specially prepared for embossing work, from the makers of the acid, and is well worth the difference in price. For flashed glass a mixture of red lead and rosin varnish is occasionally used. This is more difficult to work, does not flow so freely from the pencil, and takes longer to dry, but certainly resists the acid better than the black during the prolonged exposure to the acid and the rubbing with the mop. Rosin varnish appears to be made in several varieties, only one of which is capable of resisting acid. Red lead and japan gold size make a very reliable resist, and are therefore frequently employed to protect brilliant cut and other clear parts in triple embossing. Red lead is also occasionally added to Brunswick black for the purpose of increasing its resisting power.

WALLS.

For the wall with which the plate is surrounded to retain the acid the simplest material is pure tallow, applied by taking up a quantity on a palette knife and scraping it off on the edge of the plate. In cold weather, when the tallow becomes short and brittle, a little linseed oil is added to make it more workable. Sometimes the tallow is heated and mixed with lamp black, forming a putty which can be worked with the hands into a long thin roll. This is then pressed down with the fingers upon the surface of the plate, perhaps half an inch from the edge, if the design will allow so much margin, forming a triangular section which is very effective. The drawback to this mixture is that it has to be heated every time it is used, and it is one of the dirtiest things to handle that can be imagined. The addition of a quantity of sweet oil keeps the putty soft and does away with the necessity of heating it every time, so making it much cleaner to handle. A little working with the hands is then sufficient to put it into a proper consistency for use. The cleanest stuff to handle is undoubtedly a mixture of

Lard	...	...	...	... $\frac{1}{4}$ lb.
Beeswax	...	...	...	... 1 lb.
Canada Balsam	...	...	...	2 oz.

These are mixed by melting, care being taken that they do not catch fire, and poured into water. The mixture can then be rolled out with the hands and remains in a plastic condition, except perhaps in very cold weather. It has an additional advantage when it is necessary to apply acid close up to the edge of a plate, thus leaving no room for the ordinary wall. In such a case this mixture is worked out into a flat ribbon which is attached by one edge to the *under* side of the plate and then turned up over the edge until it stands above the upper surface far enough to hold the acid. The plate, of course, cannot lie flat upon the bench, but must be supported on blocks. The general convenience of the pure tallow seems to be so great that many workers consider it worth while to cut a plate an inch or so larger than is required in order to give room for the wall, cutting it down to the correct size when the work is finished. That is in the case of French embossing, where the acid ground comes right up to the edge of the plate— in ordinary embossing and when there is a margin of clear plate round the design the plate can be cut to the correct size in the first place.

SIMPLE EMBOSSING.

The various steps in the process of simple embossing are as follow:—First, the drawing—this has to be made, of course, full size, and in the case of lettering, coats of arms, trade marks, or any such devices which have to be seen from *outside* the building, the drawing must be reversed, as the side of the glass which receives the work is turned inwards in order to keep it cleaner than it could be if it faced weather and dust. If the devices are to be seen and read from *inside* the building the drawing should not be reversed. The plate is laid upon the drawing and the outline traced upon it in Brunswick black with either camel or sable hair pencils. The black may require thinning with turpentine, and for immediate use is best kept in a narrow-mouthed pot or bottle to prevent evaporation of the spirit. A hand-rest will be required, which should be long enough to reach right across the plate and rest upon the bench. For long straight lines the lining-pen included in most sets of mathematical instruments is most useful, as it gives when used with a straight-edge a much steadier line than can be got with a tracing pencil and works very much quicker. As these pens are generally made they are not quite suitable, being so open that they will not carry any quantity of black, and, moreover, they let it run in blobs on to the glass. This can be cured by straightening the two bent limbs of the pen with a pair of pliers, so the space between them is decreased. For use with these the black requires to have more turpentine added—the correct quantity can be easily found by experiment—and the pen should be filled by means of a brush, not by dipping it into

the black. The pen has a tendency to begin every line
with a blob, which can be corrected to some extent by
practice in handling, so a little care is needed in joining
lines. It is always best when possible to complete each
line with a single filling of the pen.

The outline completed, the groundwork of the design
(which is to become the denser, more opaque portion) is
coated with the black. Larger brushes can be used for
this—flat camel-hair in tin, for instance—care being taken
to avoid air bubbles, which are very quickly formed by any
approach to a *scrubbing* action. One is very apt, too, at
this stage to miss little bits between the strokes of the
brush and in corners of the ornament, and this must be
guarded against. Such omissions will be more easily
noticed if the plate be set up on wooden blocks an inch or
so clear of the bench. The plate must then be set aside
for four or five hours to dry, though drying can be hastened
by the application of heat. It can then be placed upon an
easel, or held up with its back to the light, to allow of
touching up the places which have been missed in filling in
or any part of the black which appears too thin to resist
the acid. After touching up it should be allowed to stand
overnight in order that the black may become thoroughly
hard.

Before applying the acid it is usual to sponge over the
exposed surface of the glass with soda water, or, in the case
of fine work, with soap dissolved in naphtha. This ensures
the removal of any grease which might otherwise interfere
with the action of the acid. The wall of tallow is now
applied to the edge of the plate, the glass being laid upon a
firm table and levelled by means of a spirit level, wedging

it up here and there if necessary. With a large plate there is naturally a tendency to sagging or bending if it be supported only at the corners, which must be allowed for. It is necessary to have the plate perfectly level—in order to use the smallest quantity of acid—to ensure the acid flowing quickly over every corner of it, and to have an equal depth of acid all over. Unequal duration of exposure to acid and unequal depth of acid will frequently affect the result to a surprising degree, though this is of course less noticeable with old, weak acid than with acid of correct working strength. The acid should be poured on to a part of the plate protected by the black ; if it falls upon an unprotected part it will be apt to produce markings of a pronounced and unpleasant character. For most purposes the correct strength of acid can be obtained by mixing two and a half parts of water to one part of acid (full strength as supplied by the manufacturer). An exposure of about twenty minutes on plate glass will give relief sufficient for grinding. Where sheet glass is used and is to be ground after aciding, three-quarters of an hour will be necessary, as the uneven surface of sheet glass increases the risk of grinding out the acided pattern. Occasionally the acid is used on obscured sheet to do away with the subsequent grinding, but in that case the etched surface is always more obscure than when clear sheet is used, though there is always sufficient contrast between it and the ground to render the pattern clearly visible.

The depth of the " bite " may be tested by " digging " with the point of a pocket knife or palette knife, but care must be taken not to displace any of the black when doing so. After a little practice the " feel " of the edge of a

FIG. 24.—Design for Memorial Window, by Wm. Aikman.

sufficiently deep bite is easily recognisable and forms a useful check against time for strength of acid.

To pour off the acid, the plate ought to overhang the edge of bench or table by a few inches. The corner ought then to be well greased on the edge and under side to prevent acid running underneath and marking the back of the plate. The gutta-percha bucket can then be held under the corner and three or four inches of wall removed with a palette knife. It will be found necessary to tilt the plate slightly in order to remove the acid—in the case of a large plate the table top should be tilted along with it to avoid risk of breakage. When the acid has been run off the plate can be swilled with water to remove the traces of acid. The black can now be cleaned off with paraffin oil, which in turn is removed with clean sawdust.

GRINDING.

The plate is then ready for grinding and should be laid upon felt, carpet, or similar material in order to provide equal support and avoid any possible scratching from grit on the bench. Grinders are made by cementing wooden handles on to pieces of plate glass from six to twelve inches square with shoemaker's rosin. The rosin is melted and poured on to the square of glass, the handle—a plain block of wood of convenient size for the hands—is pressed down upon the rosin, and as soon as the rosin cools the thing is ready for use. The plate is now sprinkled with *flour* emery (where the " bite " is deep a slightly coarser grade can be used, but increases the risk of scratching and of damaging the pattern) and water, and the grinding is done by a circular motion of the grinder, the weight of the hands being applied with discretion. Moderate weight assists the grinding—excessive weight will bend and break the plate. More emery and water are added from time to time as required. The grinder should never be *lifted* off the plate, as the suction is considerable and undue force may break the grinder, especially after it has worn thin, and leave splinters on the plate which will be apt to scratch. Always *slide* the grinder off at the edge of the plate. The time occupied in grinding is purely a question of energy. Progress can be ascertained from time to time by sponging off some of the emery and drying the surface.

Where part of the plate has to be kept clean, in addition to the " grinding line " already mentioned, it is customary to use a guide lath in the case of straight lines, bridging the plate and supported at the ends by pieces of wood slightly thicker than the plate and nailed through them to the bench. Where curves and intricate shapes have to be treated in similar fashion it will be found sufficient to use a small-sized grinder and exercise care not to work over the grinding line. When the grinding has been satisfactorily accomplished the plate should be washed with soap and water after sponging off the emery. Scrubbing with a moderately hard brush, such as a cheap nail brush, will remove all traces of emery from the etching and leave a perfectly clean, sparkling obscure.

FRENCH EMBOSSING.

The procedure with triple-embossed work is entirely different and much more complicated. If brilliant cutting enter into the design at all, that has to be done first. Then it and any parts of the design which are to remain clear are covered with the Brunswick black or, for greater safety, with red lead and japan gold size. A combination of the two will be found to answer very well. The objection to the red lead and gold size is the weight of the lead and consequent difficulty in working. Brunswick black, on the other hand, works very easily, but is not so certain to resist the very long exposure to the acid which is required in triple work. The plate is now walled in preparation for exposure to the white acid, but before this is poured on the surface is washed over with very much diluted fluoric acid. This not only cleans the surface, but helps the effect which the subsequent application of the white acid has upon the surface. The white acid is then poured on, and after having been allowed to remain for about an hour is poured off, when it will be found to have left behind it a thick white deposit. This must be removed with a rubber squeegee and clean water, care being taken not to disturb the black. As soon as the plate is dry it will be ready for the next application of the black. We now have a wide expanse of white obscure which is to furnish the high lights of the design as it will appear when seen by reflected light, and we must next proceed to cover up all those high lights with the black, tracing them from the drawing in their exact shapes. The obscure is still clear enough to allow of the drawing being seen through it.

For the next step we want *fluoric* acid, regular working strength, two and a half of water to one of acid. The plate is exposed to the action of this for *five minutes*, and No. 2 tone is reached. Then the glass is washed again with water, dried off, and black applied to those parts which have to be kept of No. 2 tone. The next exposure to acid

will require *fifteen minutes*, and will give us No. 3 tone.
Another application of black to preserve tone No. 3 and
a final exposure to acid for twenty or thirty minutes will
give tone No. 4, known as satin finish. When the black
is cleaned off we ought to find a regular and delicate gradation of tone from the dense white obscure of the white acid
to the perfect transparency of the clear plate and the
sparkle of the brilliant cutting. Viewed against a black
background by reflected light, the white acid part appears
as white, the clear as black, with the intermediate tones in
regularly graded greys. Seen against the light, this sequence
is reversed, the clear part appearing lightest and the white
acid part most dense.

Variations of Acid.

Variations of the acid in the course of working are sometimes useful. In ordinary embossing dilute acid gives a
clearer, less opaque "bite" than that of full strength, but
of course it is slower in action. A small quantity of
powdered fluor-spar sprinkled upon the surface of the
acid while it is on the plate will sink into it and render
the "bite" very much rougher. A variation of this method
produces the surface known as *stippled embossed*. Ground
mica is substituted for the fluor-spar, a small quantity being
mixed with acid (full strength) one part and water one part.
This mixture is then poured upon the plate and some more
of the mica sprinkled upon the surface. Acid once used for
this purpose must of course be reserved for it only. Each
time it is used there will be a considerable addition of mica.
The excess will settle as sediment and can be thrown away
when it becomes troublesome. Different grades or sizes

of mica will produce different effects, and can be obtained
ready for use from the Mica Lubricant Co., 63, King Street,
South Shields. The peculiar surface produced by this
process is extremely useful with gilded or silvered backgrounds for fascia plates and other advertisements on
account of the sparkle which it gives to the metal.

STENCIL WORK.

The use of stencils in embossing comes in wherever a
number of repetitions of one pattern will pay for the work
of cutting the stencils—where a number of small pieces of
work have to be turned out to one design, or where a border
has to be repeated round a large plate. Paper stencils are
in this case useless, the only practicable material being a
tin-foil specially prepared for such work and known as 4 oz.
stencil metal. It is made in sheets as large as 72 inches
by 30 inches, and costs 2s. per lb. It can be had from
Messrs. Locke, Lancaster, and W. W. and R. Johnson and
Sons, Ltd., 94, Gracechurch Street, London, E.C.

The process is of the " brushing-out " order. The glass
is first coated all over with Brunswick black and the usual
precaution of touching up observed to prevent all chance of
pin-holes, etc. The stencil is placed in position on the
glass and stuck down by means of soft soap, or, better still,
yellow soap which has been boiled to about the same
consistency. This ensures its being held in perfect contact
with the black and prevents its shifting. A brush dipped
in naphtha (a nail brush answers very well) is now rubbed
over the stencil, and almost instantly removes all black
left uncovered by the metal. This is followed by a sponge
with soap and water, which cleans away the naphtha. The

stencil is then *stripped* off the glass by lifting it gently at one corner, and the soap removed from the black with the sponge and water. A fresh part of the black is then soaped and the stencil laid down again. The operations have to be smartly performed but are really simple, and a very little practice will bring deftness of hand. In designing and cutting stencils for this work it will be seen that the aperture in the stencil represents the part of the design upon which the acid is to act. Allowance has to be made for ties in the stencil, but even continuous designs, such as Greek frets, can be stencilled by using two alternate stencil-plates, one of which will in use obliterate the ties of the other.

There is a method of applying lead-foil as a resist for embossing which in some respects resembles stencil-cutting, but with this important difference—that the foil itself is used to resist the acid and is destroyed in removing it from the glass, so that it only serves for one operation. The *modus operandi* is as follows : The glass to be operated upon is coated all over with Brunswick black well diluted with turpentine. As soon as this has become tacky a sheet of foil is laid over and pressed into contact with a roller squeegee or similar instrument. If the sheet is not large enough it may be joined by means of careful overlapping. The foil is then coated with whiting mixed with gum and water, which when dry will give a surface upon which drawing can be done with a blacklead pencil. The parts of the design to be exposed to the acid are then cut out with a stencil knife, the detached pieces of foil being peeled off with the fingers. When cutting is completed the Brunswick black still adhering to the exposed portions of the glass is cleaned off with turpentine or naphtha, and the glass can then be put under acid. The advantage claimed for this process is that it gives cleaner and more delicate detail in elaborate small designs ; for ordinary work there would be no gain in using it.

A suitable foil for the purpose, known as O. B. foil, is manufactured by Messrs. Betts & Co., 1 Wharf Road, City Road, London, E.C. It measures approximately 4,000 square inches to the lb. and costs 1s. per lb.

PRINTED EMBOSSING.

The desire to cheapen embossing by eliminating hand-work has given rise to many experiments in the direction of printed or transfer work. The utility of such must of course be more or less restricted, the varying sizes of the work making it difficult to use stock designs. Occasionally in the case of an order for a number of plates to one size the difficulty disappears, and in other instances can be over-come to some extent by using a printed centre-piece with an adaptable border which may be either printed or stencilled. With careful design and arrangement a very great deal may be done in this way. The purely technical difficulties in the way are considerable, and it has required some fifty years of experimenting to obtain really satisfactory results, the greatest trouble being in getting a clean print on the transfer paper and from the transfer paper on to the work in hand. The tendency is for the resist to spread under the pressure of printing and so give an impression with a ragged outline, which takes a great deal of touching up and scraping to clean it up—so much as almost to rival the time taken in tracing the outline in the ordinary way. The remedy for this appears to lie in the composition of the resist, which we will deal with presently.

To take the necessary steps of the process *seriatim*. In the first place, the design has to be produced in "negative" on a plate which may be either of metal or of glass. In the case of metal, etching would be done with nitric or hydrochloric acid, and the plate would be more secure against accidents, but in a glass shop it seems more natural to use glass and hydrofluoric acid, and the glass answers the purpose quite as well as the metal does. In fact, it will be found to possess at least one advantage in its perfectly level surface, which ensures that the scraper which has to pass over it to remove the superfluous resist will be in equal contact with every part, which is by no means certain in the case of a metal plate. The design then is etched into the plate in reverse, the space to be acted upon by the acid in the finished work being protected from it at this stage. When using the glass plate it will be found advisable to use the lead-foil resist described above; the cleaner the etching at this stage the more chance there is of obtaining a clean transfer later on. The etching is carried to about the usual depth attained in ordinary embossing and the resist cleaned off. Thorough cleaning of the plate at this point will help to ensure a clean transfer. The printing ink or resist which is to be transferred to the paper is then coated equally over the plate, and the superfluous quantity scraped off by means of a sharp-edged steel straight-edge which is passed over the plate, removing the mixture from the original surface and leaving it undisturbed in the etched hollows. The paper to be used for the transfer is then laid over and the plate passed between a pair of rubber-faced rollers to ensure perfectly equal contact. The paper can then be lifted by the corners and carefully peeled off. It is then laid down accurately upon the plate to be operated upon, and great care is necessary here, as shifting the paper means a smudged print. This plate is then passed through the rollers and the paper again peeled off, when the resist ought to be found adhering to the glass. Time having been allowed for the resist to harden, the plate will then be ready for exposure to the acid.

The composition of the resist varies considerably. It ought to be a mixture of resinous and greasy substances, each of which must be proof against the action of the acid. One of the oldest receipts mentions bitumen, stearine and turpentine, another one gives wax, Canada balsam and soap, and a third turpentine, asphaltum, beeswax, rosin and tallow or lard. In any case a very thorough mixture of the ingredients by the aid of heat is necessary to ensure good printing. It is probable that the exact nature of the ingredients and their proportions may be varied to a considerable extent, but it is evident that too great a proportion of the harder, more brittle substances, such as wax or rosin, will make a " short " compound which will not adhere sufficiently to both the glass and the paper, while too great a quantity of the grease—soap, stearine or tallow—will cause the mixture to spread under pressure and produce the smudgy outline already referred to. Weather and temperature also influence matters to a great extent and have to be allowed for accordingly. More grease will be required in cold weather, more rosin in warm weather, while a variation in the quantity of turpentine will frequently be found useful. Experiment can be the only safe guide, more especially because a resist which will be quite suitable for large open work will not answer for fine work.

The paper used for the transfer also varies, a thin paper coated with wax being used by some workers, while others prefer what is known as "Pottery Tissue," a paper which is used for transfer work on pottery, and which can be procured from Messrs. Wenger & Co., Hanley. If the resist does not transfer freely from the paper to the glass it can be assisted by steaming the back of the paper, by sponging it over with very dilute hydrochloric acid or by passing over it a warm iron. With the latter there is, of course, a risk, if the iron be too warm, of melting the resist and making it spread. A fresh sheet of paper will, of course, be required for each transfer.

Generally it will be found that large masses of resist do not transfer well, and this difficulty has to be guarded against either by keeping the ornament and the background very equal in extent when making the design, and so producing an "all-over" effect which is not always desirable, or by aciding only the outline of the ornament on the negative plate, printing this off by means of the transfer paper on to the work in hand, and then filling in the background with Brunswick black by hand in the usual way. Another reason for avoiding large spaces is the chance of the scraper dipping or bending into the hollow and removing too much of the resist. When using the scraper it will be found that a small amount of the resist is left upon the raised portions of the plate. This does not matter, as it will be found that it does not transfer and so will not affect the result. In any case it will be found almost impossible to clean it off without disturbing the material remaining in the sunk portions.

DESIGNING.

In designing for simple embossing the principal points to be considered are that there are only two tones at command by which any effect can be produced, and the contrast between these two is comparatively slight. A third tone can be had in the clear plate, but the use of this is generally confined to simple panel shapes on account of the difficulty of grinding to intricate forms. Probably more is made of this difficulty than need be, but triple embossing has so nearly ousted the older form for all but the cheapest work, that whenever clear glass is required in any part of the design the newer process is generally used. With only the two tones, there is still a choice left as to which shall be used for ground and which for ornament. In most cases the obscure tone is used as background and the etched tone as ornament, there being some reason for this in the fact that if the etched part is larger in surface than the other, there is a chance of the corners of the grinder dipping into it and marking it. That then has to be guarded against: relief and intaglio must be so distributed as to support the grinder at all points and ensure its passing quite level over the intaglio. Large, open ornament can, of course, be treated with a larger-sized grinder, and the use of obscure ornament on etched background might well be exploited more than it is at present. Anything in the way of shading can only be suggested by means of lines or cross-hatching, and consequently a frankly flat treatment of all ornament is most likely to be successful. Attempts at realistic devices, portraits, figures, and animals are always failures from an artistic point of view. Even if they look approximately right from one side of the glass the reversal of the tones will make them look all wrong from the other. Freedom of design, so far as outline is concerned, is untrammelled ; the acid will do anything which the pencil can.

From the practical point of view, as embossed plates are so frequently used as screens to ensure privacy, the obscure tone is generally made to predominate ; and above the eye level the clear glass is introduced to secure outlook or increased lighting.

In French embossing, instead of two or three, there are five —or, including brilliant cutting, six—tones to be considered, and the distribution of these is sometimes a matter of considerable difficulty. Where a specially obscure effect is required, the white acid will naturally predominate, and the clear plate possibly have to be omitted. It is a good general rule to lay down that one tone should always be considerably more in evidence as to extent of surface than the others in order to secure breadth of effect and repose. So, too, the masses of ornament should vary in size and should not be too equally distributed over the surface. Contrast in tones should also be considered. No. 3 and No. 4 tones placed side by side would both appear flat and uninteresting, but separated by a line of No. 1 bordered on either side with No. 5 (clear) would gain immensely in character. Always flatness of effect should be sought after. In spite of the number of tones at command, light and shade effects are seldom satisfactory. The addition of supplementary effects such as crystalline and stippled embossing has

FIG. 25.—Memorial Window. Wm, Pape, Leeds.

its drawbacks as well as its advantages. It is very easy to overdo things and make a piece of work look hopelessly showy and vulgar through over-elaboration. These two effects, when they are used with French embossing, should be used only as backgrounds for panels or cartouches, containing, for instance, lettering. They are so strong that they will throw all the softer tones completely into the shade if not very carefully handled. Gilding, silvering, and staining must be used in the same sort of way, only for lettering or other important points. I have seen a border surrounding an embossed plate very nicely brought out by a little gilding judiciously applied on the lines and corners, but, generally speaking, the gilding would be safer in the centre of the plate.

The sequence or gradation of tones can be most effectively remembered by looking upon No. 1 (white acid) as white, and upon No. 5 (clear plate) as black, with the other three as intermediate greys. The introduction of the brilliant cutting is perhaps the most difficult part of the matter—it is in itself so hard in outline and form that etched ornament surrounding it must be made to conform to it as much as possible. Where cutting appears amongst some of the clearer tones it is frequently an advantage to surround it with a thin outline of white acid. The juxtaposition of these different items, however, must always be very largely an individual matter, and the success of the effect must depend largely on the taste and originality of the designer. As is always the case, practical experience of the process is necessary to be able to obtain the best results. Too close following of tradition and of usual practice is rather a hindrance than otherwise, and at present there is every need for breaking off into original treatments, seeking inspiration and suggestion rather in other forms of decorative work than in what has been done in embossing in the past. The technical limitations of the process will of course make themselves felt at every turn, and must be frankly accepted. The resourceful designer is always ready to seize upon any apparent hindrance and turn it into an opportunity, and so the distinctive characteristics of different processes are built up.

It must be remembered that the addition of gilding (which will show to the outside) to embossed work means that it will show to the inside only as black. Where the black is of a good shape, and there is not much of it, this may not be a disadvantage, but it must be taken into consideration in preparing the design. The same remark applies equally to silvering. Yellow stain, on the other hand, shows principally to the inside, being visible on the outside merely as a semi-metallic lustre in the body of the glass, which undoubtedly enriches the effect without being in the least obtrusive. Even so, it is useful on lettering, giving just a little added note of richness and a little more separation from the surrounding detail.

CHAPTER V

BRILLIANT CUTTING AND BEVELLING

THE process which is known by the trade name of brilliant cutting is a development of the engraving process which has so long been in use for the decoration of table and other hollow glass ware, the difference consisting solely in the scale of operations, and therefore differs from the processes already described in being very largely a mechanical process. The design is cut into the surface of the glass by abrasion upon a rapidly revolving stone wheel; the rough cut is smoothed up a wooden wheel, and finally polished with a revolving brush. The handicraft which is, nevertheless, an essential part of the process, comes in the handling of the plate by the workman, who has to hold it against the edge of the wheel and turn it in whatever direction may be necessary to allow the wheel to follow the design. The effect produced, though inclined to hardness, fully justifies the name applied to it, and when the design is well suited to the peculiarities and possibilities of the process is distinctly handsome. It is at its best when sparingly used as a finishing touch to triple embossing. The process appears to have been invented, or rather evolved, in the United States, and was first worked in England about the year 1850 by Mark Bowden, of Bristol.

The machine on which the work is done is a heavy wooden

or iron frame (see Figs. 26 and 27) containing a tub, which catches the superfluous water from the revolving wheel. It is usual to keep a fair amount of water in the tub to add weight and secure steadiness, but it must be kept below the level of the circumference of the wheel to prevent its being thrown about. Between two wooden uprights, which rise one on either side of the tub, is the horizontal iron spindle bearing the cutting wheel and a belt pulley by which it is connected with the driving shaft. Adjustment of the belt is obtained by setting the "frame" nearer to or farther from the shaft. Water is supplied to the working surface of the wheel from a bucket suspended from the ceiling in a convenient position beyond the frame, trickling from a plug in the bottom by way of a piece of coarse twine to a light upright standard set on a board laid across the tub, from whence a stick conveys

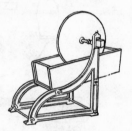

Fig. 26.

it to the circumference of the wheel. On the opposite side a piece of sponge, held against the stone by a piece of wood, distributes the water equally over the face of the stone and prevents its being thrown on to the worker's clothes.

When the glass is not too large and heavy it is merely held in the hands and placed against the wheel, but in most cases the weight is too great to allow of any freedom or steadiness in handling. Plates up to 3 feet square can be held in the hands, but a good deal will depend on the individual workman, for whereas one man appreciates the perfect freedom obtained by holding the plate, another prefers to be rid of the weight, and so obtains a more delicate

touch upon the stone.   Large plates are therefore suspended
from a kind of scale-beam having a balance weight at the
other end, so as to take the weight entirely off the worker's
hands. This scale-beam hangs from a pivoted hook
travelling by means of a wheel upon a horizontal beam
towards and away from the power shaft. The balance-
weight (about 56 lbs.) is best arranged to slide upon the

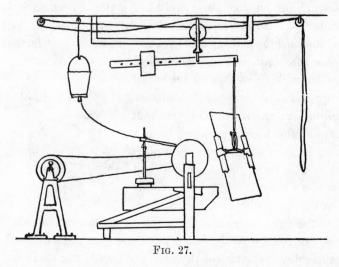

Fig. 27.

arm of the scale-beam with a pin passing through holes in
both weight and beam to fix it in the required position to
counterbalance any particular plate. From the other end
of the beam, which may be from 4 to 6 feet long over
all, the plate is suspended by an iron rod with a hook at
its lower end. A piece of soft wood, of U-section, from 1
foot to 3 or 4 feet long according to the size of the
plate, is placed over either edge of the glass, then a flat
hook over it. The two hooks are strapped together by

means of a bridle of stout rope, a travelling piece upon which is looped over the hook on the iron rod. The weight of the plate can be exactly balanced by sliding the balance weight along the scale-beam, and so the glass hangs in mid-air, capable of being moved in practically any direction by a touch of the hand. A useful addition is a cord running over pulleys at the end of the travelling beam, by means of which the whole " sling," with the plate upon it, can be moved backwards and forwards.

The stone used for the cutting wheels is a carboniferous sandstone, obtained from Craigleith Quarry, near Edinburgh, no other seeming to give the necessary combination of qualities. The discs vary in diameter from $1\frac{1}{2}$ inches to 3 feet and in thickness from $\frac{3}{4}$ inch to 1 inch. The periphery is of round, square, or " mitre " section, the latter being a very obtuse V-shape, used for " trellis " and " star" patterns. Generally speaking, a large stone is used for straight lines, and smaller sizes for curved lines—the sharper the curve, the smaller the stone. To ensure an absolutely true cutting edge the stone, after being mounted on its spindle, is set in motion and " turned "—as if in a lathe—to the required section by the application of a soft iron bar, together with sand and water, to its edge. It should be noted here that large square-faced stones for straight line work must be made with varying widths of face to suit different widths of line. As the stones are all about one thickness, it follows that both sides must be bevelled off with as long a bevel as possible in order to get the face down to, say, $\frac{1}{4}$ inch, that $\frac{1}{4}$ inch being parallel with the axis of the stone. It will also be seen that great accuracy is necessary when mounting a stone upon its spindle, by means of wooden wedges, to ensure that it shall run perfectly true, without any lateral play or " wobble." Having been brought to the required shape and size with the iron and sand, it is then smoothed down with a piece of Craigleith stone and finished off with a piece of flint.

The smoothing wheels are of willow wood in sizes corresponding to the cutting stones, ground pumice stone and water being applied to the edge of the wheel while it is in use. These wooden wheels are turned to shape with an ordinary gouge and polished with pumice stone and water. The final polishing of the cut is done on a revolving hard fibre brush 7 inches in diameter, rouge (colcothar or ferric oxide) and water being sponged on as before. The application of the pumice and rouge to these wheels is done by a boy with a sponge or a brush made of straw, the pumice or rouge being mixed with water in a bowl or other suitable vessel. All wheels revolve so that the upper part is moving *from* the operator.

When the groundwork of the design is to be obscured, the plate is first ground with emery and water as described on page 141, when the design can be outlined upon it with blacklead pencil. When the ground is to be clear the outline can be painted on with Brunswick black, well thinned down with turpentine, using the smallest possible amount of the black, merely enough to give a visible line, as any excess is likely to cause the stone to " fire." That means that the black adhering to the surface of the stone causes it to drag and jump with a fiery motion in place of its usual running, which is delightfully smooth, so smooth that the contact of the plate with it is of a very sensitive nature, and almost as much is done by feeling as by sight in following the pattern. The action of the wheel is watched through the plate from the reverse side, and the nicety of touch necessary is gradually acquired by practice. The slight drag of the stone is distinctly felt, varying with the pressure put upon it, as well as its check against the edge of the cut, which is a considerable help in steadying the plate. It might be expected that there would be a little difficulty in placing an obscured plate upon the wheel, but it will be found that the edge of the wheel becomes distinctly visible through the obscure while still an inch or more distant from the surface of the glass. The cutting proceeds more quickly than one would at first expect, but naturally narrow lines cut more quickly than broad. In the case of a broad surface it is best to move the plate about a little and so work gradually down to the full depth and breadth required. As the cutting goes on the mud formed by the water and the disintegrated glass and stone trickles down the surface of the plate, and somewhat confuses the design. On a clear plate, with outline in Brunswick black, this can be sponged off, but on an obscured plate the pencil outline will not stand sponging. A little practice enables one to follow the design correctly, in spite of these meandering streams—the plate is being continually turned in following curves, and gravitation makes them run in all directions— and an experienced workman finds them no hindrance.

A considerable amount of judgment is required in selecting suitable stones for different parts of the design, and it may be necessary to change the stones frequently to get the best effect. As has already been mentioned, large stones are best for straight lines, because the flatter curve of the cir- cumference brings more of the stone into contact with the glass without cutting too deeply, and not only makes it easier to keep a steady line, but also to cut more quickly. The large stone is, however, unsuitable for curves. On a 3-foot stone it is impossible to cut a curve of less than about 2 feet radius. So the size of the stone must be decreased to suit the sweep of the curve. The smallest curves—say a circle of 2 inches diameter—would be cut on a stone of about 6 inches diameter, and to facilitate the holding of the plate at the correct angle, without fouling the upright carrying the spindle, the stone in this case would be mounted comparatively close to the left-hand end of the spindle, the driving pulley being on the right. All parts of the design for which one particular stone is suitable should therefore be picked out and cut before changing, in order to waste as little time as possible. The square-faced stone is, of course, the most useful for all-round work, and on one of about 18 inches diameter a smart workman will be able to execute a surprising variety of work.

In cutting straight lines, whether on a square-faced or mitred stone, the plate is held parallel to the axis of the wheel, so that in the case of a square-faced stone the cut is of equal depth right across, and with the mitre face the apex of the V is exactly in the centre of the line. The mitre stone is only used for straight lines, but these may be made ray-like or leaf-like in character, *i.e.*, growing gradually wider and then narrowing again to a point, simply by varying the time during which the stone is allowed to act at any particular spot. If the plate be held motionless on a " mitre " stone a vesica-shaped spot will be produced whose length will be regulated by the diameter of the stone. Mitred stones, being used only for straight lines and such spots, are all large. Elliptical spots can be got by holding the plate in one position, parallel to the axis, on a round-faced wheel, the length of the ellipse depending on the diameter of the stone. Circular spots are cut by holding the plate parallel to the axis of a round-faced wheel and revolving it slowly in the plane of its own surface.

In cutting curved lines, which are always done on square-faced stones, the plate is held not exactly parallel to the axis of the wheel, but at a slight angle with it, so that only one edge of the stone cuts into the glass, and not the whole width of the face. So it is possible to cut lines of varying widths, the groove being deep on one side and bevelling away to nothing on the other. This deep side is always on the *inside* of the curve, for mechanical reasons which will be readily appreciated, and in an ogee, or S-shaped curve, half of the curve is done on one side of the stone and half on the other—or if it be more convenient to keep to the same side of the stone the plate is turned end for end—the meeting of the two showing a " scarf "-like joint. In cutting lettering and complicated ornamental shapes these joints can be turned to very good account, as their facets add to the brilliance of the effect, but if not neatly made they may look very objectionable.

When a plate with an obscured ground is undergoing the polishing process. the brush frequently goes beyond the edge of the cut, and polishes to a greater or less extent part of the background, giving a soft and cloudy instead of a clear and firm outline. This is remedied by regrinding the plate after polishing is completed. One is tempted to ask, Why not defer the grinding until after polishing in that case ?   There are several reasons.   First, the design is more easily outlined on the obscure ground than on the clear ; second, the action of the wheel is more easily seen ; third, the cutting would have to be deeper if the whole plate had to be ground subsequently.

Though the stone wheels, wood wheels, and brushes are interchangeable upon one machine, it is advisable to have more than one machine available, in order to save constant changing. The least number of stones with which any variety of work can be done is about four, of 6 inches, 12 inches, 18 inches, and 24 inches diameter respectively, but with this number it would be necessary frequently to turn down the edges of the stones to round-faced or mitre, according to the nature of the work in hand.

Power for driving the wheels can be obtained from gas, oil, or steam engines or electric motors. Where the sand-blast is also in use the steam engine will naturally recommend itself. An electric motor is specially desirable on account of its silence, the small attention which it requires, the small space which it occupies, ease in starting, economy in lubricating oil, etc. The gas engine will be useful where electricity is not available. As a final alternative an oil engine, such as the "Diesel" (a vertical engine, burning heavy oil, with flash point above 73° Fahr., and very economical in working), will give excellent results. The horse power required may be from five to ten. Six brilliant cutting frames and four bevelling machines can be driven with 5 h.p., but as it is always advisable to have some power in reserve, it is much better to have 10 h.p. for such an equipment. The four bevelling machines will take perhaps twice as much power to drive them as the six brilliant cutting frames, on account of the greater weight of the wheels and the heavier pressure put upon them in working. The two processes are practically inseparable, though many a plate may have to be bevelled without having any brilliant cutting upon it, and *vice versâ*, and it is very unusual to lay down plant for the one without the other.

The driving shaft requires to run at about 160 to 200 revolutions per minute, and its most convenient position is about 3 feet above the floor. This arrangement requires only a short belt to connect the shaft with the machines, and also keeps the belt quite out of the way of the sling, which therefore has greater freedom of movement. When the shafting is suspended from the ceiling it is necessary to use a long belt at a very considerable angle to keep it clear of the sling. A vertical belt is quite impossible for this reason, besides giving no opportunity of tensioning the belt by the simple expedient of shifting the frame. A driving shaft in this position does not perhaps give the most economical arrangement of floor space, but the loss in this respect is comparatively small, and the advantages in other respects will easily counterbalance it.

BEVELLING.

For bevelling the edges of plate glass the outfit is somewhat larger than for brilliant cutting. Whereas in the latter case all the operations can be performed on one frame by changing the wheels, in the former case three, or even four, separate machines are necessary. In all of these the discs revolve in a horizontal plane instead of vertical. The first has a flat cast iron wheel about 30 inches diameter by 4 inches thick; the second a stone wheel of the same dimensions and of a softer material than the Craigleith stone used for the cutting stones; the third and fourth wheels of willow wood (same size), which may be made interchangeable on one machine, but are better, for all the difference in first cost, to be separate. On the first the rough grinding is done with sand and water, the second is for smoothing, on the third the smoothing is carried a stage farther with the aid of ground pumice stone and water, and on the fourth the final polishing is done

Fig. 28.—Bevelling machine with stone removed.

by means of rouge. All of these machines have a bad habit of throwing mud and water centrifugally all over the place, which is curbed to some extent by a shield. Round half the circumference this shield rises some inches above the surface of the disc, but on the other side it has to be kept an inch or so below the surface to allow free access for the glass, and there the spray is uncontrolled.

No sling is used to carry the weight of the plate in this case. When the glass is of extra size it is held by two or more men, one of whom directs the work and keeps the plate at the proper angle with the wheel. No gauges of any kind are used, the operator merely testing the width of the bevel from time to time with a foot-rule. The wheels have been spoken of as flat and horizontal to distinguish them from the brilliant cutting wheels with which the work is done on the circumference. The working surface of the bevelling wheel is its upper horizontal surface, not the circumference, and this surface is not perfectly flat. There is a hollow of a foot or more in diameter in the centre which practically converts the wheel into a *ring* with a working face 9 inches wide in the case of the iron wheel, 4 inches wide on the stone wheel, and 2 to $2\frac{1}{2}$ inches on the wood wheels. This working face slopes outwards and downwards from the horizontal at a very slight angle—just so much that the edge of a large piece of glass in contact with the wheel on one side is lifted quite clear of it on the other. The wheel revolves " with the sun," and the glass is applied to the *right-hand* side of it, so that the wheel is always *coming* towards the edge of the plate. The reasons for this arrangement are as follow : Although the surface of the wheel is not accurately horizontal, it is, to all intents and purposes, practically so, and it is infinitely easier to keep the plate at the required angle with it than it would be on the circumference of an ordinary grindstone, besides having a larger surface of contact, and, in the second place, the edge of the plate is presented to the revolving wheel in order to prevent accumulation of sand or pumice stone, which would naturally take place if the wheel revolved in the other direction, and which would scratch the surface of the glass beyond the edge of the bevel.

The sand and water required on the cast iron wheel for the initial grinding are supplied from a large conical iron hopper which hangs above the wheel and allows the mixture to drip directly on to it. This sand may be of practically any character which is easily obtainable. The pumice stone and rouge are applied to the wood wheels by hand, as already described in the case of brilliant cutting.

Fig. 29.—Staircase Window for Shipping Office,

The sandstone wheel does its work with no assistance save that of water, which is allowed to drip on to it from a pipe by means of a tap.

Straight edges of plates are bevelled upon these wheels without trouble ; rectangular notches in shaped plates and convex curves can also be done ; but concave curves have to be worked in the first place on a cast iron wheel of 30 inches diameter by 1 inch thick, and with a round face, mounted vertically in a brilliant cutting frame. This has its attendant sand-and-water hopper in the same way as the horizontal iron wheel. The smoothing and polishing of these curves is done on ordinary brilliant cutting wheels.

Rounded edges on plate glass shelves are obtained by means of a brilliant cutting wheel with a grooved circumference. Square edges on shelves, etc., are ground on a stone of ordinary grindstone pattern about 18 inches by 4 inches mounted on a brilliant cutting frame.

The bevelling machines, having vertical spindles and driving pulleys set only a few inches above the floor, cannot be driven direct from the same shaft as the cutting machines, but require extra gearing, which must be arranged as may be necessary to suit the size and shape of the workshop, etc. Machinery for brilliant cutting and bevelling is to be obtained from Mr. Edward G. Rider, of Pott Street Ironworks, New Islington, Ancoats, Manchester, who makes a speciality of machinery for glass working.

POLISHING.

It will be found an advantage to have available a polishing machine by means of which scratches, acid marks, and other stains or blemishes may be removed from a plate.

Such a machine is illustrated in Fig. 30. It will be seen that the rubber is carried by a jointed arm, which admits of its being easily moved over the whole surface of a plate, so that it will work equally well in any corner without any adjustment. The rubber block itself has a universal ball joint, which ensures perfect contact with the

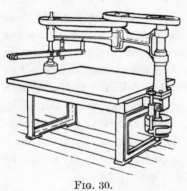

surface of the glass, and is faced with felt to which a mixture of rouge and water is applied. The block has a rotary motion, to which a back and forward movement can be added by hand, while the pressure of the block upon the glass can be regulated in the same way. The machine is entirely self-contained, re-

FIG. 30.

quires no special fixing, and can be driven from the same shaft as the bevelling machines.

DESIGNING.

The knowledge of the peculiarities of the process required in designing for brilliant cutting is even greater than in most other glass processes, for the simple reason that its possibilities are fewer. Ornament capable of being cut upon the wheel is practically confined to that of a line and spot character. Palmated and foliated work, except in so far as they can be suggested by lines and spots, are impossible. A "line" may be widened out to $\frac{3}{4}$ inch or 1 inch, but a clear surface larger than that, though it could be produced, would have no effect, except, perhaps, on an obscured ground.   At least as much brilliant cutting is done on clear plate as on obscured, and its effect on the clear plate is due entirely to the contrast produced by the angle which the cut forms with the surface of the glass. When the cut is a wide one that angle, unless the cut be exceptionally deep, is reduced to practically *nil*, and the effect is lost.   Ornament of the brushwork type frequently met with on Greek vases is very suitable for reproduction by cutting, while "key" borders and similar fret patterns are very practicable.   Foliated ornament built up of a number of forms resembling brush strokes can be carried out successfully, but is seldom attempted.   It would, of course, entail a great deal of work and turn out proportionally expensive.   Circular and elliptical spots are easily produced; square and triangular blocks, up to 1 inch side, by means of four and three cuts respectively.   Trellis and star patterns are so easily produced and are so very showy that they form almost the entire stock-in-trade of the cheap worker, but they have little claim to artistic effect.   Circles near the centre of a plate are easily produced, but circles near the edges or corners are more troublesome.   In such cases the plate has to be swung round on an axis which coincides with the centre of the circles to be cut.   If that centre be right in the corner of a plate measuring 5 feet or more across the diagonal, the farther corner of the plate has to describe a circle of nearly 10 feet diameter in turning.   The movement of the plate is of course a very slow one, and there is ample opportunity for the workman to alter his hold upon it, because there is no necessity for carrying the cut right round at one sweep, so it is not impossible to cut circles in corners, but it is certainly very awkward and consequently very slow. The workman holding the plate should have his hands as near the point at which cutting is going on as possible, but at the same time they ought to be near the centre of gravity to have proper control of the movement. Large curves are comparatively easy to work ; the difficulty increases as the radius decreases.

The limit of size for brilliant cut plates is generally about 5 feet square, that being the largest plate that can be handled with safety and efficiency by one man. Slightly larger sizes can sometimes be worked by two men, but unanimity of movement is difficult. Plates as large as 8 or 9 feet have been tackled where a small amount of cutting—straight lines and spots—has been required to enhance the effect of embossed work.

One of the pitfalls into which a designer is apt to stumble in this process is that of monotony in width of lines, size of spots, etc. Contrast should be introduced as freely as possible, wide lines alternating with narrow, large spots with small, and so on. Owing to the swinging of the plate on its centre point as it hangs on the sling, there is a tendency to confine ornament to the centre of the plate and to make it more or less radial in character. This is perfectly practical and in keeping with the requirements of the process, but a too frequent use of it becomes monotonous, and it is well to get away from it when possible, especially when a plate is small and easily handled. Designs of a simple nature, capable of being cut without much turning of the plate, can be placed above or below the centre. Simplicity of design in this connection does not necessarily mean a minimum of work. A number of straight lines and spots can be cut more easily than a few curves, and the necessity for change of wheels is also a consideration.

With regard to lettering, which is frequently required for shop-door plates, etc., practically any character of letter can be cut, but that of a " fish-tail "—half-Gothic—nature is most easily cut and is very showy. Letters with pointed serifs come next, while plain block letters are the most difficult. Script letters look well, and are fairly easy to execute.

Design for brilliant cut work has so far followed too closely along certain accepted lines. There is ample opportunity for the introduction not of really fresh elements, because, as has already been stated, the capabilities of the process are limited, but for their adaptation and rearrangement into combinations which will make even greater use of them and show them off to greater advantage. This is to be done not by trying to do what has been done on other and more tractable materials, but by beginning with the simplest elements of what the process can do, and from them building up a style of design which shall be peculiar to the process itself, and which may yet be thoroughly good and interesting ornament. The difficulty in the way of accomplishing this very desirable object is that so few designers have any practical experience of the actual work, and so few cutters have sufficient knowledge of design to enable them to turn their actual experience of the work to account.

The difficulty of handling the plate is the greatest drawback to the process, becoming quite insurmountable in the case of large plates. If it were possible to have the plate laid upon an easel or a bench and handle the wheel as a hairdresser does his revolving brush there would be no limit to size, and it would be as easy to cut a curve in the corner of a plate as in the centre.   Any such simple arrangement as his elastic india-rubber driving band and hand-held spindle is of course out of the question.   Handling a 3-foot cutting stone would be worse than handling a 5-foot plate, and any arrangement of jointed arms, on the principle adopted in polishing machines, would become tremendously complicated and expensive before the necessary range of movement was attained.   There would also be a difficulty in seeing exactly what the wheel was doing, which under the present arrangement can be seen with perfect ease from the back of the glass.   The use of smaller stones would, of course, simplify matters, and both the mechanical and the visual difficulty might be met in this way.   If any satisfactory method can be devised by which the wheel may be moved instead of the plate the scope of the process will be very considerably enlarged, while the risk and waste of time involved in handling the plates as at present will be considerably reduced.

CHAPTER VI

THE sand-blast is the most recent of the more important processes used in glass decoration, and has probably not yet reached its full development, though considerable progress has been made with it since its discovery. It had its origin in observation of the fact that on sandy, stormy coasts the windows of buildings near the beach are scratched and dulled by sand blown against them by the wind. In many places windows have to be reglazed annually on this account. Although this action of the sand had been noted for centuries, it was not until 1870 that the knowledge was turned to account and the same result produced mechanically by Benjamin Chew Tilghman. After a few primitive, but nevertheless highly satisfactory, experiments, he patented in every civilised country a process for working hard materials with a blast of sand, driven by air pressure, the first English patent being No. 2147 of 1870. The air blast was produced by a fan and the air fed into an ascending pipe at a short distance from its upper end, while the sand entered the same pipe from a horizontal branch. If a plate of glass was moved about at a distance of about an inch from the upper end of the pipe it was uniformly obscured in about half a minute.

In 1873 a fairly perfect, although complicated, sand-blast machine was exhibited at Vienna and created much excitement and astonishment by the rapidity with which it produced many decorative effects. Nevertheless, the sand-blast process was no exception to the great rule that the hardest part of a task was the beginning of it. One of the greatest difficulties met with at first was the production of clouds of minute siliceous dust which had a most destructive action upon the lungs, and cost many workmen their lives. Another difficulty was to find a coating for the glass which would resist the blast, and so render possible partial etching for the production of patterns. All sorts of glue and other compositions were patented, to the benefit of the Patent Offices alone. Miller, in his work on the sand-blast, recommends paper stencils, but the day of paper stencils, except for small work, has long gone by. The first real advance was made when zinc stencils were used, either as a direct protection to the glass, or as a means of printing and transferring.

The sand may be used wet or dry, and in various degrees of fineness. The fineness of the grain produced on the glass is directly proportional to the fineness of the sand. The finest sand produces a matt very similar to that obtained with French acid. Only *sharp* sand is of any use —sand from a river, or from the sea-shore, is useless, as it has been so rounded by the action of the water as to have no cutting edges. Dug sand may have been rounded by water in some past geological period. All fresh supplies of sand should therefore be tested on a waste piece of glass, or by microscopical examination, preferably by the former method. Reigate sand is the sand chiefly used for the purpose in this country. The opening through which the sand issues is made of various sizes, and the blast can be made to impinge upon different parts of the glass, either by moving the glass or by moving the blast nozzle.

In using the sand-blast, the oldest arrangement exposed the glass openly to the action of the sand. It is now, however, enclosed in a chamber which prevents the escape of the fine siliceous dust so detrimental to the lungs of the workmen. The blast may be produced in six different ways: (a) by atmospheric pressure, obtained by creating a vacuum in the etching chamber; (b) compressed air; (c) by a combination of (a) and (b); (d) by steam; (e) by centrifugal force; and (f) by the action of gravity.

In the centrifugal method, the sand falls vertically upon a rotating wheel, carrying buckets on its circumference. The wheel rotates at a high speed and throws the contents of the buckets in succession upon the surface of the glass. The blast is directed either horizontally or vertically. The finest grain is got with wet sand, which requires, however, a higher velocity than dry sand. In using the steam blast there is a danger of the glass being cracked by the heat. It can, of course, be kept cool by passing water over the side on which the blast is not acting, but a much better plan is to make a current of air pass between the glass and the blast opening. This sweeps the steam away, but is of such strength that it has no appreciable effect upon the motion of the sand. The steam blast itself may be made to produce the air current by well-known methods, or the current may be produced independently. If the air is heated in its passage it can be made to free the sand from moisture.

The sand-blast machine, as generally employed, requires, as has been stated, a blast of air or steam, and the apparatus is unsuitable for the production of small quantities of work on account of its size and cost. The idea naturally arose that it might be possible to design a machine of small size and price if, instead of the artificial blast (the means of producing which forms the chief item in the cost of the ordinary machine), the necessary velocity were given to the sand by gravitation, *i.e.*, by allowing it to fall from a height. The process was successfully worked out by an American named Morse, who found that, if the sand were mixed with a harder substance, a comparatively small fall would give the mixture the necessary abrading power. Morse's machine consists simply of a wooden box which is kept supplied with sand from a hopper. From the box the sand falls down a vertical tube about eight feet in length, and reaches the glass from a small jet. It is found that under these circumstances a paper stencil is a sufficient protection for the glass, strong paper being used and secured in position by pasting. When the paste is dry, the stream of sand is started, and the glass is held under it and moved about so that the sand comes into contact with every part of the stencil in turn. Care is, of course, necessary that the blast is not allowed to act longer on one part than on another, for in that case the pattern would not be cut into the exposed parts of the surface of the glass to a uniform depth, or to a uniform matt appearance. Both flat and curved surfaces can be etched with a matt pattern on a smooth ground with great rapidity and in faultless style with the Morse machine. Some judgment is required in making the mixture in the hopper. For very hard glass a mixture of carborundum and emery should be used instead of sand. For softer glass a mixture of sand with either of these substances can be used, and for engraving on metals the machine acts perfectly well with sand alone.

The Morse machine has the disadvantage that the sand which has acted on the glass has to be constantly removed, or it will interfere with the action of the stream. The best practical method is to have a sand receptacle at one's elbow, and to repeatedly sweep the sand off the plate into it. This, if done quickly with a turn of the wrist, does not waste very much sand, or lengthen the duration of the process seriously.

A foot-blower with an air reservoir such as is used for large blowpipe work can be used to produce the air current for a sand-blast. The best arrangement is to let the air blast escape from an inner nozzle surrounded by that from which the sand is driven. The suction draws up the sand so that it rises in the annular space between the inner and the outer nozzle, and is driven out by the blast.

Stencils are most frequently used, either as a direct means of protecting parts of the glass from the action of the sand and so producing a pattern, or as a means of applying a resist, such as india-rubber, which shall fulfil that function. The method of preparing the stencil will, of course, vary according as it is to be used for the first or the second of these two purposes—in the first case that part of the design which is to appear matt on the glass will be represented by a perforation in the stencil; in the second case the arrangement is reversed and the matt part of the design will be solid in the stencil. In either case the stencil may be cut out with a sharp knife or a graving tool, but it is not unusual to make metal stencils by etching them. One method of doing so is as follows :—On a zinc plate, about $\frac{1}{50}$th of an inch thick, the design which is to be etched upon the glass is painted with a brush in a composition made by melting together asphalt 10 oz., beeswax 12 oz., Venice turpentine 10 oz., turpentine 10 oz., tallow 3 oz., diluted when cold to a working consistency with turpentine. Those parts of the stencil which have to be perforated are left unpainted. When the coat is perfectly dry the other side of the zinc is painted all over with the same composition in two coats, letting the first dry before the second is applied. A wall of wax, tallow, rosin, and powdered asphalt is then put round the patterned side of the zinc to form a shallow dish. This dish is then filled with dilute nitric acid—one part of ordinary commercial 1·4 S.G. acid to three or four parts of water—which at once attacks the exposed parts of the zinc. While the acid is acting the bubbles of hydrogen which are formed must be cleared away with a very soft brush. Care must be taken not to have the acid too strong, or so much heat will be developed that the protecting composition will be softened and become useless. Observation must be kept upon the temperature, and if it is found that the plate is getting warm, the acid should be poured off until it is quite cold again. Fresh acid must then be applied, as the old lot will not act properly again. In the course of from sixty to ninety minutes the zinc is usually perforated. When this is the case, the acid is at once poured off and the border removed. The composition is then washed off with turpentine or paraffin and soap and water, and any deficiencies in the etching corrected with a file. For cheap work the stencils are sometimes stamped out with steel dies, in which

Fig. 31.—Triple Embossing.
Wm. Pape, Leeds.

case they must be again rolled to ensure their being
properly flat.

Stencils cut from tinfoil, paper, wood-fibre, etc., are
used as a means of applying rubber and other similar
resists, and these materials have the advantage of being
easily cut with an ordinary knife. The minute detail which
can be cut in these materials by a practised hand is sometimes surprising, and they are on that account frequently
more useful than zinc and other metals.

A transfer method is very useful for preparing a number
of stock stencils to one pattern. A sheet of steel, copper, or
zinc about one-eighth of an inch thick is procured, and the
design etched upon it as a negative—*i.e.*, those parts which
are to be perforated in the zinc stencil to be prepared from
this sheet are left untouched. The etching should not
penetrate the sheet deeper than $\frac{1}{50}$th to $\frac{1}{40}$th of an
inch. The sheet is then rolled with composition, and
a print is taken from it with paper. The composition is
then transferred by means of the paper to the thin zinc
which is to form the stencil, and which is then etched as
already described. In making the thick stock pattern sheet
the etching, to a depth of $\frac{1}{50}$th of an inch, takes from
fifteen to thirty minutes. The printing composition is
made as follows:—yellow wax 10 oz., asphalt 10 oz.,
powdered talc 10 oz., Venice turpentine 5 oz., rosin 5 oz.,
turpentine 10 oz. If this is too stiff to print with, as it
may be in cold weather, add more turpentine. In applying
the paper after rolling on the composition care must be
taken that it is neither creased nor stretched. When it is
in position, a roller like those used by photographers for
mounting photographs is passed over it to get rid of air

bubbles and ensure perfect contact. To remove the printed paper take a sponge dipped in warm vinegar and wet the paper all over. It can then be removed without affecting the composition, so that another print can be taken.

It is evident that stencils can be made from other metals than zinc if a suitable mordant is employed. The following are two recipes for etching steel, which is largely used in sand-blasting :—(1) Commercial hydrochloric acid and water in equal volumes; (2) acetic acid one gallon, methylated spirits one quart. For copper use nitric acid mixed with its own volume of water.

The stencils, as has already been mentioned, may be used either as the direct protection or merely as a means of applying a protective composition. The best protective composition for resisting the sand-blast is india-rubber, but on account of its high price other materials which will resist a few exposures are substituted for it in most cases. The usual practice is to employ thin stencils of mild steel. Whatever the nature of the protective composition may be, if the stencil is to be employed merely as a means of transferring it to the glass the stencil is firmly fixed upon the glass, and the composition is applied by means of a kind of squeegee of sheet iron or hard wood which is dipped into the stuff and drawn over the stencil. The squeegee should carry neither too much nor too little of the composition, and the stencil should lie absolutely flat upon the glass. The glass itself is prevented from moving by bearing against stops fixed in the table, which must not project above the glass so as to prevent the squeegee from passing over them. After applying the composition the operator sees that all the openings in the stencil are completely filled with the resist, supplying any deficiencies with a small palette knife. He then lifts the stencil off the glass with a steady hand, lifting it by one edge slowly and gradually while the opposite edge is kept fast against the stops. Half an hour afterwards the glass is usually dry enough to be blasted. It should be carefully examined first, however, to see if the stencilling has been properly done and that all the outlines are perfectly sharp. If there are any faults, a skilled hand can generally put them right with a fine brush and some of the india-rubber composition. The rubber is, of course, supplied in the form of solution. There are many recipes for this resist, some of which profess to be secret. As a matter of fact they are all solutions of raw (unvulcanised) rubber in naphtha or any of the usual solvents. What the glass etcher uses is the same product as is employed by the cyclist as rubber solution, but for sand-blast work only the purest rubber is of any service. After the work is finished the rubber can be scraped off with a palette knife as far as possible, and the glass is then cleaned with naphtha or carbon-disulphide. For simple work where only shallow cutting is required, paper coated with a mixture of four parts of glue to one of glycerine is occasionally used. A mixture of glue and dextrine is also sometimes used as a resist without paper and can be applied through a stencil in the same way as the rubber.

If the zinc stencil is left on while the blast is operating it may itself be protected with india-rubber, and two, or even three, coats may be necessary. Before applying the stencil to the glass, all india-rubber which may have lodged in the perforations must be cleared away with a small sharp knife, so as to leave the design quite sharp and clear.

Properly painted, a stencil can be used five hundred or even a thousand times before requiring repainting. As the sand-blast is so frequently used for the production of cheap advertising showcards in flashed and other glasses, these large numbers are not unusual. The stencil is firmly fixed to the glass plate by small clamps. To do this, of course, both stencil and glass must be approximately of the same size. In elaborate and expensive work, however, it is usual to stick down the stencil with cement. As the cement is not exposed to the blast, any cheap adhesive may be used.

The resisting power either of a stencil or of a protective composition, when exposed to the sand-blast, depends upon its being soft and elastic and yielding to the impact of the grains of sand. Such substances as india-rubber and lead are therefore excellent protectives. Cast iron plates, on the other hand, even a fifth of an inch thick, are rapidly destroyed. Wrought iron stencils last about four times as long as those of cast iron of the same thickness, but metal stencils require frequent renewal unless protected by india-rubber or asphalt varnish. It is remarkable, as showing the peculiar quality required of resists for this work, that cotton lace resists the sand-blast sufficiently well for several pieces of glass to be blasted to a pattern with the same piece of lace as a stencil. The lace must, however, be gummed on with common gum, so that any of the adhesive which spreads on to the parts to be matted may come off freely under the blast, and so not impair the uniformity of the matting of the exposed portions of the surface. In the same way, if fine sand is used at a low pressure, ferns and similarly delicate objects will resist long enough to be used

for patterning the glass.   Letters cut out of paper and
blackened with an asphalt or coloured rubber varnish stand
the blast fairly well—well enough to be left on if the desired
effect requires it.   In any case they can be touched up with
more varnish in any place where they may have been
damaged.   They must, however, not be fixed on with
ordinary gum or glue, but with paste or marine glue, or
they will flake off under the blast.

The use of the stencil naturally has its limits, with
regard to the character of the designs which can be
produced by its means.   For small or complicated designs
with minute details the stencil cannot be properly cut, and
there are many designs in which it would be impossible to
arrange for the "ties" necessary to the existence of a
stencil.   Neither does the stencil admit of gradation or
shading.   Of course it must be clearly understood that
shading as generally understood is impossible with this
process.   The grain of the matt can be rendered coarse
or fine by the use of varying qualities of sand, but nothing
like the variation of tone possible in French embossing can
be attained here.   Shading can only be achieved by means
of lines, cross-hatching, etc., and these, to be effective, will
naturally be somewhat too fine for stencil work.   Recourse
must be had, then, to printing by means of the paper
transfers already described from etched steel plates, which
are prepared as follows.   The pattern is painted on the
steel with Brunswick black or an asphalt varnish, applying
the colour to the background only if the pattern is to be
transparent, and *vice versâ*.   If the ground is to be dull, as
soon as it has been painted in, the outlines only of the
pattern are put in, and then shaded places in the pattern

—*i.e.*, places where the background is to show. In the reverse case the pattern is painted in without any break, and shades are put into it by scratching parts of it so as to láy bare the steel underneath, somewhat after the fashion of copperplate etching. Fine shading is impossible, as these streaks, whether of asphalt or of bare metal, must be at least $\frac{1}{50}$th of an inch wide.

It is clear that on etching the steel plates the painted parts, whether ground or pattern, will remain in relief. The etching must not be more than $\frac{1}{50}$th of an inch deep, for if the protective composition reaches more than that height above the rest of the plate it will crush in the press, and the pattern will be smudged. The plate is rolled over with the rubber or other protective composition after etching and washing off the asphalt, and makes either a positive or a negative as the case may be. All the stopping is now shaved off with a spatula, except what is in the depressions. A paper is then laid on it and covered with two or three thicknesses of cloth. The whole is then put in a press, and the pattern is thereby printed on the paper, which is then put, printed side downwards, on the glass to be blasted, and rolled to bring every part of the stopping into contact with the glass. The print on the glass will be dry in about an hour, and the paper is then removed with a sponge dipped in lukewarm water or in vinegar. The plate can be blasted as soon as dry. By this process practically any design can be worked with perfect freedom, as the printing does away with any necessity for a stencil character in the design, and finer work all round can be done by it.

Although the sand-blast will not give a smooth surface, but always a matt 'ground it is constantly employed when

deep hollows have to be cut in glass. In this way a species
of *intaglio* work can be produced upon thick plate glass
which when viewed from the reverse side gives the effect of
relief. This is done, of course, in several operations, each
successive portion of the design being " stopped out " when
it has reached a sufficient depth. These hollows can be

FIG. 32.

polished by means of emery
and rouge, should a transparent effect be desired.

The most useful machine
for all - round work is that
manufactured by Tilghman's
Patent Sand Blast Company,
Ltd., Broadheath, near Manchester, specially for glass
work, and illustrated in Fig.
32. This machine is worked
by steam, $3\frac{1}{2}$ horse power of
steam at a pressure of 20 to
25 lbs. per square inch being
required, but perfectly adequate means are provided for
separating the steam from the sand so that no undue
heating of the glass is experienced. The machine stands
$3\frac{1}{2}$ feet high, and the blast is delivered in a vertical direction from an aperture of about 4 inches diameter in
the top of it. The glass to be operated upon is held
face downwards over this aperture and moved about as
may be required. The limit of size of glass which may be
worked in this way will naturally be about 3 feet square,
though this may be exceeded by having two men to handle

the glass. For large plates it is best to use a compressed air apparatus with flexible blast pipe, somewhat after the fashion of a fire-hose. The plate can then be set on edge against the wall and the blast directed against any part of it by means of the flexible tube (Fig. 33).

The first machine is so much enclosed that there is no necessity for making any special provision to guard against the dust produced, but in the second case the work has to be done in an enclosed room, and the operator must wear a helmet somewhat after the style of a diver's helmet to protect him from the clouds of sand. This helmet is provided with an air tube carrying a supply of air from the air compressor sufficient to provide adequate ventilation.

Compressed air machines similar in design and size to the steam-blast machines described above can be had, but they are more expensive to install because of the cost of the compressor which is required in addition to the boiler which supplies the blast direct in the case of the steam machine.

" Crystalline " Glass.

Crystalline glass is produced by the application of glue to the surface in a liquid condition, the powerful contraction of the glue as it dries tearing away the surface of the glass and leaving a surface marking similar to the effect produced by frost upon window panes. The marking can be produced over the whole surface of a sheet of glass, or it can be confined to particular parts of any desired shape, and so combined with embossing or sand-blast work, giving an extra variety of surface.

A great deal depends on the kind of glue used, Irish glue seeming to give best results. To prepare it for use a

FIG. 33.

quantity of glue is placed in a vessel with sufficient water
to cover it and allowed to soak for twenty-four hours. If
in that time all the water has been absorbed or evaporated,
more should be added, as it is essential to the success of
the process that the glue should contain as much water as
possible. When the glue has absorbed as much water as
it will take, it should be liquefied over a water bath—the
ordinary pattern of glue kettle will answer—and will then
be ready for use.

On a polished glass surface the glue will take no hold,
and it is therefore necessary to roughen it in order to get a
grip. This can be done by means of sand-blast or grinding
with emery, the former being, of course, cheaper where it is
available. Where it is desired to confine the crystalline
effect to a certain area, it is advisable to outline that part
with Brunswick black in order to obtain a firm, clean outline and prevent any chance of the glue spreading beyond
it. The surface must be absolutely clean and free from
grease, which would prevent the glue from holding, and the
glass must be laid quite level upon a bench to ensure an
equal coating of the glue. The liquefied glue is then laid
on with a wide brush, a good thick coating being necessary
to ensure success. As soon as it is sufficiently dry the glass
is removed to a room which can be heated to a temperature of
95° or 100° Fahr. There it is allowed to remain until it
is perfectly dry, which will mean a period of from ten
to twenty hours. As the glue contracts in drying it
frequently begins to chip away the surface of the glass,
but this does not always happen, and it is occasionally
necessary to give it a change of temperature in order
to produce the desired effect. This is simply done by

removing the glass to a cooler room, but it must be remembered that there is a risk of breakage in doing so. The contraction of the glue is in many cases so violent as to break thin glass, such as sheet, especially if there be any tendency to convexity on the side upon which the glue is applied. Plate glass, generally speaking, on account of its thickness, is safe from this risk. The change of temperature will generally bring the glue away completely, and as it flies into the air in chips the workman must look out for his eyes. It will be found that the working of the process is considerably affected by changes of weather.

The crystalline marking may be made larger and more open by applying stout paper—brown paper, for example—over the surface of the glue while it is still wet. The paper should be thoroughly damped before applying, but should contain no superfluous moisture. It will thus have a considerable shrinking power of its own, and, by preventing the glue breaking up into such small pieces, will produce a larger pattern. When this process is used in conjunction with embossing or sand-blast it will be found best to do the glue work first, so that in case of breakage as little work as possible may be wasted.

The character of the marking varies with the quality of the glue, with the weather, temperature, etc., and it is never safe to predict exactly how it will turn out. Occasionally the process is repeated a second time in order to obtain a stronger marking. It is sometimes used on flashed glass, with the result that the coloured veneer is partly removed, and the small portion of it which is left shows up the crystalline pattern very strongly.

CHAPTER VII

GILDING, SILVERING, AND MOSAIC

GILDING upon glass is used principally in sign-writing and decorative work of a similar character, and is also occasionally applied to embossed and brilliant cut work for the purpose of giving added prominence to lettering and other salient points in the design. The process consists of applying ordinary gold leaf to the back of the glass with a transparent isinglass or gelatine size which allows the metal to come into very close contact with the glass, and the effect thus obtained by adding the high polish of the glass surface to the natural brilliance of the gold is very handsome. The process is rather a delicate one, demanding neatness of hand and considerable practice, but is not at all complicated. The gold is fastened to the glass in the first place by the size, but has to be further secured and protected by a backing of varnish and paint to protect it from damp and give it any degree of permanency. It can, of course, never have the same claim to permanency as if it had been fluxed upon the glass by firing in a kiln, but well-executed work has stood the test of twenty years and more without deterioration, and for most purposes for which it is used is perfectly satisfactory.

The *sine qua non* of good gilding on glass is *absolute cleanliness*—unless the surface be clean and free from every suspicion of grease the size will not flow freely upon it, and the gold will consequently fail to adhere. It may occasionally be necessary, in the case of an old piece of plate glass, to go over the surface with a weak solution of nitric acid, followed by clean water, but in the case of new glass less drastic measures will suffice. In the case of gilding upon embossed plates it will be necessary to make sure that every suspicion of the Brunswick black resist and the paraffin which has been employed to remove it has disappeared, and a scrubbing with soap and water is advisable in order to do this, though the nitric acid might be equally effective. The strong point about the scrubbing-brush method is that the bristles of the brush will penetrate into all the corners of the embossed work. Brilliant cut work has been so polished in its final process as to require comparatively little cleaning.

The size used is made from the finest *Russian* isinglass as follows:—Place a small teaspoonful of isinglass in a clean jug and pour over it a pint of boiling water. Cover the jug with a saucer and allow it to stand in a warm place for about twenty minutes till the shreds of isinglass dissolve. It is sometimes useful to add a small quantity of pure spirits of wine — about one-and-a-half tablespoonfuls to the pint. This helps in clarifying the size, and is also useful if there should be any trace of grease upon the surface of the glass. Many workers consider the size incomplete without some quantity of spirit, while others refuse to admit that it has any beneficial effect whatever. In the same way there is a difference of opinion as to whether the size should be used warm or cold to obtain the best results. The present writer has always been quite successful when using the size cold, and it is evident that to keep it warm would cause quicker evaporation and consequent alteration of strength, though possibly the exact strength is a matter of little moment.

In sign-writing and similar work, where there is no embossing, the gilding is generally done first, all outlining, background, and other painting work being done afterwards, but when embossing is introduced to enhance the quality of the gold the embossing comes first, gilding next, and painting last. When used in conjunction with embossing and brilliant cutting for window work and without any paint (except backing), gilding is the last step in the work. When gilding embossed work the etched outline forms a convenient guide both for applying the gold leaf and for trimming away the superfluous gold afterwards. If there is no embossed outline a reversed drawing must be used as a guide, and tacked on to the face side of the glass with gum or other adhesive, so as to show the reversed shapes of the ornament through the glass towards the back, the gold being applied to the back of the glass. The glass is then laid, back upwards, upon a level bench, and the farther side tilted up to an angle of about 20 degrees to prevent the size when freely applied from lying in too deep a pool on the surface.

A gilding cushion, knife, and tip will be required to apply the gold leaf, which for glass work should be of a special quality prepared for the purpose, carefully selected as to colour and placed in books without any of the red bole powder which is generally used to prevent its adhering to the paper. This gold leaf must not be stored in any place where it is likely to be affected by damp, as that would cause it to adhere, and therefore spoil it. A number of

Fig. 34.—Triple Embossing. Wm. Pape, Leeds.

leaves of gold are dropped one by one from the book within
the parchment screen at the end of the gilding cushion and
are brought forward one by one to be flattened out, cut up,
and transferred to the glass, the cushion being held palette
fashion on the left thumb. The handling of the delicate
leaves at this stage is almost impossible to describe, and
differs in no way from the regular practice of gilding upon
other materials. The leaves have been dropped in a more
or less crumpled condition on the cushion—they must on
no account be touched by the fingers. The knife is delicately
inserted under the uppermost one, when it will be seen that
the crumpling is to some extent an advantage, affording the
knife easier entrance. The leaf is gently lifted from the
heap, brought forward to the open end of the cushion, and
laid down as flat as possible. By breathing gently upon
it, it may now be flattened out perfectly smooth, but any
excess of blowing may play havoc with the other leaves.
Most beginners find this a most awkward business—the
slightest breath seems to disturb the little pile of gold, an
unintentional cough or sneeze will free the leaves from
their parchment prison and send them floating broadcast.
In the effort to control his breathing the tyro comes near to
suffocation. Once flattened out, the leaf can be cut to any
required size. The knife, which to all appearance is too
blunt to be of much use for cutting, is placed firmly on the
leaf and moved gently backwards and forwards once or
twice. Too great a pressure must be avoided as being apt
to cut the leather of the cushion. The knife must be kept
clean and free from grease or rust—grease will make it
stick to the leaf and tear it, and rust will have a similar
effect. The tip—a very thin flat brush of camel or badger

hair mounted between two thin cards—is then used to lift
the cut pieces of gold and transfer them to the glass. It is
laid gently upon the surface of the leaf, which will adhere
lightly to it. If it does not adhere it may be necessary to
add an infinitesimal quantity of grease to the hair of the
tip. This is efficiently done by merely brushing the tip
lightly upon the hair of the operator's head, but must not
be attempted by gentlemen who are fond of hair oil. The
gold can then be deposited in position upon the glass, which
has already been coated with the isinglass solution by
means of a large camel-hair flat brush. Care must be taken
to prevent the tip becoming wet with isinglass. If the size
be lying too deeply upon the glass, the leaf will have a
tendency to float downwards, which can be corrected by
touching it lightly with the tip, moving it into position and
holding it there for a second or two till the excess of the
size has drained from under it, when it will hold its place
without farther trouble. Apart from this little difficulty, the
glass cannot be kept too wet. The size must not be allowed
to dry until all the gold is in position, because in drying
the isinglass gathers more thickly on the edge of the pool of
solution. Should it be allowed to dry, it must be moistened
again so as to entirely obliterate this line of demarcation,
which would otherwise appear as a flaw on the surface of
the gold.

In gilding complicated ornament it is a mistake to cut
the leaf into very small pieces for two reasons—the small
pieces take so much longer to apply in the first place, and
are more likely to require patching afterwards. At this
stage the shape of the gold can only approximately correspond to the form of the design. The main point to be

observed is that all points of the drawing are covered, the result being a comparatively shapeless mass of gold from which the true shape will be evolved later on. Each piece must be laid so as to slightly overlap its neighbour to secure a solid effect. Work will begin at the top left-hand corner and be continued towards the right and downwards, applying fresh size from time to time to ensure keeping the surface properly wet. When the gold is all in position, the glass must be allowed to dry. When all trace of moisture has disappeared, the surface can be gone over with a very soft pad of cotton wool to remove any loose particles of gold from the overlaps and to burnish the whole. This must be done very lightly, though firmly, in order to avoid scratching the gold. It is usual then to flood the surface with hot water in order to once more dissolve the size, ensure its perfectly equal distribution, and remove any excess. The water is applied with a large wash-brush of camel-hair, which must be brushed over the surface so rapidly, so lightly, and with so full a charge of water as to avoid scratching the gold. No part of the gold must be gone over twice, or scratching is inevitable.

The glass, having dried once more, is ready for second coating or for patching. Second coating is advisable where very high-class work is required, but for average work one coat carefully looked over and patched will be sufficient. Patching may be found necessary at the overlaps and occasionally along the outline of the ornament. Whether for patching or second coating, the previous process is repeated, except that now the size has to be applied over the first coat of gold, and therefore greater care is necessary. In patching, the size should be used sparingly, applying it only on the spots where it is required, for fear of its running below the gold and drying there with cloudy edges. In second coating the size should be applied over only a small space at a time to avoid any risk of moving or damaging the first coat. The washing will not be necessary after the second coat, and burnishing can be done as soon as all the water has dried off.

The drawing must now be taken from below the glass and "pounced," by pricking holes with a needle along the outline close enough together to show the line clearly, the paper being laid upon two or three thicknesses of cloth during the pricking. The drawing is then laid over the gilding in exact position, and a pounce bag of coarse calico, which has had its stiffening washed out of it, filled with lamp black or powdered chalk, is dabbed upon the paper, the lamp black or chalk passing through the pin holes and so transferring the design to the gold leaf. We now have a guide by which the shapeless mass of gold can be brought into shape.

After this point procedure differs according to circum-stances. When a design is simple or largely composed of straight lines, as in block lettering, "trimming" is done next. This consists of outlining the ornament by removing the superfluous gold with the point of a hard wood stick (lancewood, for instance, used by carriage builders for carriage shafts) and making a clean-cut, sharp edge to the whole design. Straight-edges are used wherever possible, and for curved lines a mahl-stick or hand rest is employed to steady the hand. When the whole design has been out-lined in this way, the first step towards fixing or backing is taken. Colourless varnish is applied by means of a tracing pencil to the edges of the ornament in a line about $\frac{3}{16}$ inch wide, $\frac{1}{8}$ inch of which will be on the gold, the remaining $\frac{1}{16}$ inch on the background. This provides a transparent and therefore invisible protection to the edge of the gilding, warding off the attacks of cleaning cloths, etc. When this outline has hardened, the body of the gilding can be painted over. For this black japan is frequently used, but where the work has received only one coat of gold the black is apt to show through and spoil the colour of the leaf. Chrome yellow mixed with japan gold size will help the colour of the gold rather than otherwise, and is therefore preferable. This backing colour ought to come close up to the edge of the gold, overlapping the varnish, but not extending on to the transparent part of it. When the backing colour is dry, any of the gold which may still be left beyond the trimmed outline can be washed off with a pad of cotton wool dipped in water.

Where ornament is complicated and full of intricate curves and detail, a different procedure may be adopted. Instead of trimming with the hard wood point, the backing colour may be painted on first, following the outlines of the pounce, and filling in the whole bulk of the ornament. When this colour has set, the gold remaining uncovered can be washed off. The outline of the ornament is then trimmed at any point where the pencilling may not have been sufficiently neat or steady, after which the varnish outline can be applied. This is the more expeditious method, but cannot be relied upon to produce quite so clean an outline as the other.

The gilding of a large, plain background, in sign-writing, for instance, is a matter which presents many difficulties, and is so seldom thoroughly satisfactory that it is not often attempted. The essentials to its success are, first, thorough cleanliness, both of the glass and of the size; second, perfectly equal application of the size; third, proficiency in the application of the leaf, which can only be gained by practice (the leaf should be applied *whole*, in order to make as few joints as possible); and last, very careful burnishing to hide the joints. Only the specially selected leaf should be used for this work to avoid variation in colour. A method which appears to be particularly successful employs gelatine size in place of isinglass—best French gelatine. This is made in thin sheets which measure about 10 inches by $3\frac{1}{2}$ inches, and a fourth part of a sheet dissolved in one pint of hot water gives the correct working strength. Before applying the size the glass is treated to a bath of pure alcohol to ensure freedom from grease. Sizing and gilding then proceed in the usual way. Second coating proceeds as soon as the first coat is dry without any intermediate washing. When the second coat of gold is dry, the whole is carefully burnished with cotton wool. The size is now doubled in strength—half a sheet of gelatine to a pint of water—and has pure alcohol added to it in the proportion of one tablespoonful of the spirit to a pint of the size. This mixture is now applied as a protective coating over the gold to prevent the oil or varnish in the backing colour from penetrating the metal and affecting its colour. Work done by this method appears to show none of the cloudiness so often observed in work done with isinglass, and approaches very nearly in appearance to gilding done by depositing processes.

A plain gold background, however, almost invariably

looks poor and cheap, and for this reason it is frequently enriched with a diaper etched by hydrofluoric acid, which has the effect of concealing the joints in the gilding in a very remarkable way and very considerably enhancing the appearance of the work. The part of the glass acted upon by the acid becomes, of course, slightly obscured and so produces a slight matt effect upon the gilding. A matt effect somewhat similar in character—something between the respective densities which would be produced by fluoric acid and white acid—can be very easily obtained without the use of acid. To do this the glass must first be coated with finely-ground whiting and water. This is frequently merely rubbed on with a sponge or rag, producing a very streaky effect, which is cleared and reduced by the succeeding work until it is not noticeable to the ordinary observer, but it is always visible to the expert. It can easily be smoothed out by the use of the badger softener, a small quantity of gum arabic being added to the whiting if necessary to make it work better under the brush.

The outline of the matt parts is then lightly pounced on to the whiting, and they are pencilled over with japan gold size, slightly thinned with turpentine. If it is too thin it will not give a clean edge. As soon as this is dry, the whiting which has not been covered up is washed off and gilding proceeded with. This is frequently used on lettering so that the body of the letter is matt with a burnished outline, and in a similar way on ornament. It is, of course, clearly distinguishable from acid work, because of the absence of the fine, bright line which marks the edge of the " bite."

Shading and fine internal lines on gilded ornament

are sometimes suggested by means of what some glass gilders call "etching." This is merely a matter of scratching or hatching the gold leaf by means of a hard wood point so that the background may show through the openings. The effect, when well used, is very good, but no attempt at anything like realistic shading should be made. The same caution applies to the use of colour, such as burnt sienna applied to the glass before gilding. It frequently happens that the work is seen in such a light that the brilliance of the gold is lost while the colour shows up very hot and unpleasant. It may be remarked here, with regard to combination of acid work and gilding, that the deeper the "bite" the more brilliant will be the effect of the gilding, because of the increased prominence of the edge of the bite.

Silver leaf can be applied to glass in the same way as gold by means of isinglass, but, on account of its greater weight and stiffness, requires somewhat different handling. Tips containing a greater quantity of hair are specially made for the application of silver leaf. It will also be found that on account of its greater thickness it is somewhat more difficult to cut upon the cushion than gold. It is made in leaves $4\frac{1}{2}$ inches square (the standard size of gold leaf is $3\frac{1}{4}$ inches square), and if stocked for any time has to be protected from exposure to air, which is apt to tarnish it round the edges and render the greater part of the leaf useless. Once placed upon the glass and protected by the backing, it is, of course, safe from this risk, and on this account can be used more freely upon glass than, for instance, upon a wooden signboard.

"Peeling" is a fault to which glass gilding is rather

prone, and seems to be caused by damp dissolving the isinglass. The only way to guard against it is to secure ample ventilation behind the glass. Signboards, etc., backed with wood should have apertures left to admit of a free circulation of air, so that any damp or steam may be carried off before it has time to cause trouble.

Gilding can be fixed upon the surface of glass by firing in a kiln in the same way as ordinary stained glass. This is done in the case of small surfaces—small lettering, etc. —by means of the gold paint prepared for gilding upon china. This can be bought ready made, but it is expensive, and the glass painter will find it an advantage to prepare his own, which can be done as follows :—A solution of gold in aqua regia (one part of nitric acid with two to four parts of hydrochloric) is precipitated by potash or green vitriol, producing a finely-divided brown powder consisting of metallic gold. This is washed, dried, and rubbed up with the flux—anhydrous borax. The two are then mixed with turpentine or gum water and applied with a tracing pencil. A clean new pencil should be used, and any intrusion of dirt or foreign matter of any kind carefully guarded against. Firing must be done at a lower temperature than is required for most glass colours, but just on that account there is always a doubt as to the permanency of the process. Overfiring will produce blistering and coppery brown stains which entirely destroy the effect. The only satisfactory means of treating larger surfaces appears to be that invented by Mr. Walter J. Pearce and described under the heading of Mosaic.

A process of gilding glass by chemical deposition has been described as follows, but seems to partake more of the nature of a laboratory experiment than everyday workshop practice. Pure chloride of gold is dissolved in water, filtered and diluted to such an extent as to give 15 grains gold in 20 quarts of water. This is rendered alkaline by the addition of soda. In order to reduce the gold chloride, alcohol, saturated with marsh gas (methane) and diluted with its own volume of water, is used. The result is the deposition of metallic gold and neutralisation of the freed hydrochloric acid by the soda. In practice, to gild a plate of glass, the object is first cleansed and placed parallel with a second plate slightly larger than itself, $\frac{1}{10}$th of an inch separating the two. Into this space the alkaline solution is poured, the reducing agent being added immediately before use. After two or three hours the gilding will be found to be fixed and the plate may be washed.

PAINTING.

Painting in oil colour on the back of plate or sheet glass for sign-writing, etc., presents no special difficulty. Tube colours are best for the purpose and should be thinned with varnish only, though a little turpentine may be added in the case of large backgrounds. Ordinary routine is naturally reversed—lettering, ornament, outlines, and shading are done first, and backgrounds last. Stencils can be used for the repetition of ornament, and pounced drawings are very useful. Backgrounds are painted in imitation of marble, wood, mosaic work, etc. It is necessary to keep all paint as thin as possible to diminish risk of peeling. Large flat backgrounds should be stippled with a good-sized stippler to prevent any show of brush marks. Oak graining may be done as follows :—The glaze which is to show the combing and figuring is applied first in sharp colour, turpentine and gold size or varnish, and combed while wet. As soon as this is dry a slightly contrasting colour is used to paint in the figuring. This is followed by wiping out the figure as may be necessary with a soft rag in the usual way. The whole must now be left to dry thoroughly before the ground colour is applied. The ground colour should be made up principally with gold size, very little turpentine being added, and applied smartly with a soft brush, all unnecessary rubbing being avoided for fear of disturbing the work beneath. Mahogany graining is generally done with a distemper colour made up of burnt sienna and vandyke brown, with stale beer as binder. This is applied in the usual way for mahogany graining, and when dry is backed with a ground colour, in which dry colours are mixed with boiled oil and very little turpentine. The fewest possible number of coats must be used to avoid peeling. In the same way imitations of marble are produced by pencilling in the "veins" first, any clouding or shading next, and the ground colour last of all. A great deal of work is done in sign-writing in which glass is used, though often but slightly. Stamped letters, of sheet copper, gilded, are cemented to the back of a plate of glass and surrounded by a painted background. Incised wood signboards are covered with plate glass for the sake of the greater brilliance, better protection from weather, and greater ease of cleaning which is afforded by the glass as compared with varnish or French polish.

The cutting of glass letters out of opal and other glasses for affixing to windows is generally done by means of the sand-blast, and they are decorated by gilding and other means. Letters cut out of clear glass are gilded on the back ; opal letters have their edges gilded, and so on. To fix these to a window it is necessary to set out on paper a full-size drawing of the whole and gum this to the inside of the window in order to show the exact position of each letter. The cement used for glass letters is usually white lead mixed with gold size, applied only round the edges of the letter, and should not be too stiff. The letter must be carefully pressed into close contact with the glass and is supported during the drying of the cement by the application of gelatine lozenges. These are cut in two in order to give a straight edge, moistened in the mouth, and stuck on to the plate about the lower part of the letter so as to prevent its sliding downwards by its own weight. For metal letters either of the following recipes may be used :—Copal varnish, 15 parts ; drying oil, 5 parts ; turpentine, 5 parts ; liquid glue, 5 parts. Mix these ingredients together thoroughly, and make up to a stiff cream with powdered slaked lime. Dissolve 1 oz. of caustic soda in 5 oz. of water, stir in 3 oz. of powdered resin, and boil for a few minutes. Make up to a stiff cream with plaster of Paris and use at once.

MIRROR SILVERING.

Previous to 1840 mirrors were silvered by means of a process which employed an amalgam of tin and mercury, first used in Venice in 1317. This has now been entirely supplanted by the nitrate of silver process, which is varied in details by different manufacturers and under different circumstances, but still remains the same in principle. A solution of nitrate of silver is mixed with a solution of

FIG. 35.—Door Plate. White Acid, Brilliant Cut and Bevelled.
Designed by A. L. Duthie.

Rochelle salt and poured upon the glass, when the silver is precipitated in metallic form. The process is a simple and, if certain precautions are observed, an easy one.

The room in which the work is carried on must be kept absolutely free from dust—this being rendered somewhat easier by the quantity of water used in the process, tables and floors being always more or less wet. There must be available an unlimited supply of *distilled* water, which must be produced from a still in which the worm is made of *pure tin*, in order to prevent any chemical contamination of the water which would interfere with the brilliance of the silver deposit. For the same reason the water discharged from the still should be stored in earthenware jars or some receptacle of a similar nature. It must not be brought into contact with iron or other metal.

The depositing process is carried out on a wooden table, whose size may be regulated by the average work required. This table must be dead level, and so arranged with hot water pipes underneath that it can be heated all over to a regular temperature of 70° to 80° Fahr. The water for these pipes can be supplied from the boiler of the distilling apparatus. Around the edges of the table is arranged a gutter by means of which all water used in washing off and all excess of silver solution are carried to a vat in which they are stored in order that waste silver may be recovered. In the same way, the blankets with which the table is covered to prevent scratching the glass, the aprons worn by the workmen, and leathers used in polishing off are periodically destroyed for the sake of the silver which they absorb.

Absolute cleanliness—chemical cleanliness—of the glass

surface is essential to a clear unclouded deposit, and the utmost care must be taken to ensure it. It should be noted here that polished plate glass, immaculate as it may seem, has a right and a wrong side. The side which first undergoes the polishing process, and which has to lie face downwards upon the plaster bed while the second is operated upon, suffers to some extent from exposure to the wet plaster and the heat generated by the polishing. It requires the eye of an expert to distinguish the two, but the chances are that if the "first" side were silvered instead of the "second" the clouding would be apparent to others. Until the eye has been sufficiently trained to discriminate between the two sides it is advisable to test the glass by means of samples. In some cases it may be useful to make matters certain by calling in the aid of the polishing machine and running over with rouge the side of the glass which is to be silvered. The polishing machine illustrated in Fig. 30 is in any case a useful accessory in a silvering shop to remove occasional small faults. It is even possible by its means to freshen up an old plate, slightly scratched by constant cleaning, sufficiently to enable it to be silvered, though generally the game is hardly worth the candle.

The right side having been fixed upon, the glass is very thoroughly cleaned with whiting and ammonia. It is then rubbed over with a solution of chloride of tin—about 1 oz. to two gallons of distilled water—applied with a piece of felt. After this cleaning, which should be done away from the silvering bench, the face of the glass must on no account be touched—the least finger touch will leave a grease mark and interfere with the silver. To remove the plate to the silvering bench it must be lifted in a horizontal position by placing the hands underneath it.

The following may be taken as an approximately correct formula for the preparation of the solutions for ordinary work : Dissolve 4 oz. of pure silver nitrate in one gallon of distilled water; then add carefully, a little at a time, strong ammonia, until a brown precipitate has been formed and redissolved, stirring the solution all the time with a glass rod. In another vessel dissolve 12 oz. of Rochelle salt (potassio-tartrate of soda) in powder in one gallon of distilled water. (Crystals, in a smaller quantity, were originally used, but a larger quantity of the powder has been found to be equally effective.) Immediately before using the two are mixed, two-thirds of the silver solution to one-third of the salt. In pouring the mixture on to the glass it is, of course, advisable to do so as quickly and cleanly as possible—splashing and uneven flooding mean waste. The depth required is just so much as will lie on the plate; it is not necessary to provide any wall on the edge to ensure depth. Along the edge, or in places where the solution does not run freely enough, it is permissible to spread it with the finger, so long as the dry finger does not touch the surface of the glass.

The rate at which the silver is deposited depends largely on the heat of the table—the higher the temperature the quicker the deposit—but the best results are usually obtained with 70° to 80° Fahr. Depositing is generally complete in from half an hour to an hour. The plate is then swilled with distilled water to carry off the solution, and very carefully mopped over with chamois leather soaked in the water to remove any roughness and give a certain amount of polish. It is then removed from the depositing bench and placed upon another bench or upon trestles for the painting or "backing" process. As the silver coating is still too delicate to stand the friction of a paint brush, it receives a first coat of shellac dissolved in methylated spirit and thin enough to be poured on. This dries very quickly and is succeeded by a backing of red lead, Indian red, or other colour made up with turpentine and japan gold size.

Under certain circumstances, a solution of 1 lb. of loaf sugar in one gallon of water is used in place of the Rochelle salt solution.

MOSAIC.

Mosaic work in glass for mural decoration is to be met with in many different guises, varying from pure *tessera* work in opaque glasses to work in small set patterns of a tile character, to painted work such as Opus Sectile (described on page 222), and to work in transparent, or at least translucent, glasses which have been gilded or painted on one side so as to afford a reflecting surface. Opaque glass suitable for tessera work is made by a number of makers in a very great variety of colours and in all thicknesses. There are two different methods by which mosaic work is done. The old plan was to coat the wall with cement and stick the tesseræ into that while it was still soft, and this procedure, which is undoubtedly best, is still followed for important work. It has the advantage of being done *in situ*, where colour effects, etc., can be studied under actual local conditions and every allowance made for position and lighting. Another little point, important as springing from the nature of the material, is that the tesseræ are set, not with a regular smooth surface, but in apparently haphazard fashion at a multitude of different angles, so that they catch the light from different directions, and so add a sparkle and depth of colour which could not be otherwise obtained. This is especially useful in the case of gold. The second method is the workshop one, in which the tesseræ are fixed face downwards, by means of stiff paste, upon brown paper on which a reversed version of the design has been drawn. The tesseræ being self-coloured, the colour effect can be watched equally well from the back. When the paste has dried, the sheets are applied to the cemented wall, and the paper washed off after the cement has set. In this case, of course, the intelligent tilting of the tesseræ is impossible, and though it is possible to give them a poke here and there through the paper, that can serve no real purpose. The first method is undoubtedly the best for important work, but where economy has to be considered the second will be found very satisfactory on the whole. The first system necessitates the use of a slow-setting cement of a putty-like nature, such as a mixture of putty, white lead, and red lead, whereas for the second a quick-setting cement is more useful. In both cases a dark red will be found to be the most useful colour for the cement, a considerable amount of which must necessarily show between the tesseræ, and has therefore to be considered as part of the colour scheme.

The cutting up of the sheets of glass into tesseræ is effected sometimes by means of the diamond. In other cases the pieces are simply broken off with a pair of wire-cutting pliers. Much depends upon the thickness, surface, etc., of the glass in use. Some makers supply the glass cut into cubes ready for use.

The use of glass cut to shape and forming a design thereby somewhat after the fashion of a leaded light without the lead has certain advantages over tessera work, for instance economy—the cutting and placing of the shaped pieces occupying much less time than the setting of the tesseræ—and a certain amount of gain in clearness of design, owing to the elimination of the breaking-up lines except where they are really necessary to the design. On the other hand, it can never have the richness of surface and the special character always associated with mosaic work *pur sang*. This process is covered by a patent held by Mr. Walter J. Pearce, of Manchester, who gives it the distinguishing name of " Vitrémure." The points specially covered by the patent are (1) the use as mosaic of ordinary sheet glasses of various makes cut to irregular shapes, and (2) the backing of the glass with stoved enamels, metal foils, and fluxes. The special novelty is the use of metal foil protected by enamel on the back of the glass as well as on the front, and the use of the glass cut to templates instead of in tesseræ. The process is not so much an invention as an adaptation of several known methods of work to a different purpose. The most novel part of it, and the most valid part of the patent, is the use of gilding with ordinary gold leaf protected by a transparent vitrifiable enamel. By this means squares of gilded glass $3\frac{1}{4}$ inches by $3\frac{1}{4}$ inches (standard size of gold leaf) can be produced somewhere about 50 per cent. cheaper than by the Italian method usually adopted for gold tesseræ backgrounds. The constitution of the enamel with which the gold is protected is secret, and it would appear to be the only material with which it is possible to lay a leaf of gold on ordinary cathedral glass, cover it with enamel, and fire it without loss of lustre, as the least deviation from the exact recipe is fatal to the result.

American opalescent glass, with its haphazard marking in various rich colourings streaked with milky white, is particularly useful for work of this nature, and produces some very fine effects. Opalescent antiques, in which the opalescence is much less marked, are particularly fine when backed with gold, which seems to give them some of the "imprisoned fire" characteristic of the opal itself. Muffled, rippled, and other glasses with figured surface make very interesting backgrounds when gilded in this way, especially as the colour of the gold can be modified by the use of various tints of glass.

CHAPTER VIII

PROPRIETARY PROCESSES

THE Electro-Copper Glazing Process, worked by the British Luxfer Prism Syndicate, Ltd., 16, Hill Street, Finsbury, E.C., has many distinctive features. In its most characteristic form the H-section calm used in leaded lights is replaced by a narrow ribbon of copper, representing merely the heart of the lead without any flanges. This having been built up with the glass by hand, the missing flanges are added by means of an electro-depositing process, and the entire frame becomes one homogeneous piece of copper possessed of strength and rigidity so great that saddle-bars can be safely dispensed with even in large-sized windows.

By this process is produced a fireproof glass which has been tested by the British Fire Prevention Committee and accepted as fireproof by the fire insurance companies, the London County Council, and other public authorities. The glass used for this purpose may be of various characters—plate glass, " Luxfer prisms," or some of the ornamental rolled glasses.

An H-section of copper is also used for more ornamental work, giving an effect somewhat similar in appearance to leaded lights. This is made in several widths, of which only the narrower can be used for intricate work, the wider being too rigid to bend except in wide, simple curves.

Copper can also be deposited by this electro process on ordinary leaded lights, stiffening the panel to some extent, and giving an appearance of uniformity which the contrast in colour between lead and solder is apt to destroy. It is an excellent substitute for the gilding so frequently used on leaded work, being more legitimate, more permanent and less expensive.

The process of putting together the copper frame ready for the depositing process is very similar to that used in leaded lights. The ribbon of copper which takes the place of the heart of the lead varies in width according to the thickness of the glass it encloses, being so arranged as to project very slightly above the surface of the glass. This ribbon is set up on edge between the pieces of glass, the panel lying flat upon the bench with laths to keep it in position. The copper surrounding the outside is of a square U-section, of great strength for its weight, which is lapped over at the corners, while the interior ribbons are carried through slots in this outer frame and bent over. All joints are then lightly touched with solder to keep them in position until the depositing process makes all properly secure.

The electro-depositing work is carried out in large tanks, containing a solution of copper sulphate in which the panels are suspended, and the electric current required to effect the deposition is supplied by a dynamo. When a panel is suspended in this tank, copper is slowly deposited upon the edges of the ribbon until it is built up into a sort of dumb-bell section. This copper is deposited in such absolutely close contact with the glass as practically to convert the whole into a solid mass, and where the glass is of uniform thickness the cementing necessary in leaded work is dispensed with, it being claimed that the panels are wind and water tight without it. With the H-section, however, which is used with glasses of varying thickness, cementing is necessary to render it quite weather-proof.

The lightness and rigidity of this copper frame as compared with lead are very remarkable—the ease with which large panels can be lifted and handled is quite surprising—and on this account it is possible to glaze large windows without the use of saddle-bars, although T-irons are necessary to enable the lights to be broken up into lengths of about 7 feet for convenience in handling.

In the matter of design the process has practically the same capabilities as lead work, the difference being mainly in width of line, though when H-section copper is used it cannot be bent with quite so much freedom as a narrow lead. Whereas lead cannot be worked with any degree of safety less than $\frac{3}{16}$ inch wide, the copper at less than $\frac{1}{8}$ inch wide is perfectly rigid. It follows that where fine lines are required the copper has a decided advantage, and the absence of saddle-bars will doubtless appeal to some people. Exactly the same glass is used as in lead lights, and where quality of design and colour is equal the advantage would appear to lie with the copper glazing. Its greatest drawback is that of price, the cost being double that of leaded lights.

A vitreous enamel process which has many good points peculiar to itself is worked by the Sand Blast and Ceramique Company, Ltd., 3 and 4, Howard Buildings, Central Street, London, E.C. The enamel is floated upon the surface of the glass so thickly that after firing it gives a relief of nearly $\frac{1}{8}$ inch, and is suitable for carrying out designs of an arabesque character and for lettering. Being opaque, it is not suitable for effects of transmitted light, but is excellent for exterior decoration of windows and advertising purposes. Designs can be outlined in gold or ordinary glass tracing colour, or the enamel can be finished without outline. In the latter case, as an outline of some kind is necessary to keep the enamel in position when it is floated on, lamp black mixed with gum and water is used, but totally disappears in the process of firing. The gold used for outlines is similar to that used for pottery. The process is of French origin, and was protected by a patent which has now expired, but it is worked only by this firm, and the exact composition of the enamels is naturally secret. Considerable variety of colour is obtainable, mostly light tints. Firing is done in an ordinary glass kiln at about the usual temperature.

The patented process used by the Cloisonné Glass Company, 40, Berners Street, London, W., takes its name from the resemblance it bears to Cloisonné enamel. On a sheet of clear glass, which may be sheet or plate according to circumstances, the outlines of the design are indicated by flat wires standing on edge. These may be black, gilded, or silver, and are made in twelve different sizes. The spaces between these are filled with small pieces of coloured or white glass, cube-shaped, spherical, or merely broken up. These small pieces are cemented to the back plate by a transparent cement, and being pot metal, colours are quite permanent. It is usual, in order to obtain a dirt-resisting surface, to place another piece of clear sheet glass over all, securing this to the back plate by means of a binding of tinfoil at the edges, but this covering sheet can be dispensed with. Owing to this triple layer of glass, the whole is considerably heavier than lead lights, but it has greater strength and is not easily broken. Where a breakage of the cover sheet occurs, repair is a very simple affair; when the back plate is broken, it is possible to remove the coloured beads and the wires to a fresh piece of glass and make good the whole at a cost of about 10 per cent. of the original.

The most distinctive point of the material is that, owing to the number of small surfaces presented to the light, it is almost equally effective by either transmitted or reflected light. As compared with stained glass or leaded lights it does not transmit quite so much light as they, but has a great refractive power. On the other hand, whereas stained glass and leaded lights lose their effectiveness when viewed by reflected light, Cloisonné glass retains some of its colour and general character. Transparency, of course, the material in itself does not lay claim to. When transparency or a maximum of light is required, the background of any particular design can be left clear by the simple expedient of leaving out the glass beads, such a treatment being specially effective in designs of an Adam character.

The freedom of design possible is infinitely greater than in lead work, there being no arbitrary lines necessary, and the outlining cloisons being so thin as to be a negligible quantity. The range of colour is practically unlimited, the glass beads being made in over 800 tints, many of which are opalescent. Very great variety of texture is also possible. The beads are made in sixteen different sizes from about $\frac{1}{4}$ inch diameter down to $\frac{1}{64}$ inch or less; the cubes range from about $\frac{1}{4}$ inch to $\frac{1}{16}$ inch; the "granulated" or broken stuff also varies in size; so that even when using only one or two colours it is possible to secure interest by means of varying texture. Broad black lines in imitation of lead or iron work are got by using granulated opaque glass.

Owing to being visible by reflected as well as transmitted light, this process naturally lends itself to many other uses besides windows. It is used for decoration of furniture and for wall mosaics, as well as for fire screens, lamps, etc.

Opus Sectile is the name given to a process worked by Messrs. Powell & Sons, of Whitefriars Glass Works, London. It may be described as standing half-way between tile painting and stained glass. The material used is an opaque glass of a peculiar nature in which the ingredients appear to be only half vitrified. It is made in slabs of about $\frac{1}{4}$ inch thick, the bulk of the slab being coarse in quality and grey in colour, and bearing on its surface a thin coating of a finer quality in a variety of colours. The ingredients of which this glass is made are sifted into moulds in powdered form and fired in a kiln, from which they emerge in the slab form. These slabs are capable of being cut with the diamond with as much freedom as ordinary antique glass, though requiring a little more care in handling. They are then painted with enamel colours, and fired, at a somewhat lower temperature than ordinary glass, in the gas kiln. Silver stain is used on the whites in the same way as on transparent glass. The process is largely used by Messrs. Powell for reredos and mural monument work in churches, and figure designs, similar in character to stained glass windows, are executed in it. The

colours are mostly pale, and the texture of the surface
somewhat similar to that of a large, coarse egg-shell. The
pieces of which the design is composed are affixed by means
of cement to the wall of the building, and the whole is
generally enclosed in a species of niche or canopy work of
marble or alabaster, with occasionally the addition of a
little mosaic work in gold and colour. In design it is subject to much the same restrictions with regard to outline,
shapes of pieces, etc., as leaded glass, only the outline is
not so broad and heavy, there being only the heart of the
lead, so to speak, to consider, and not the flanges.

"Marmorite," the property of the Decorative Marmorite
Company, 55, Queen Street, London, N.W., is a process which
is suitable for mural decoration, but not for windows, the
result being perfectly opaque. The material itself is an
opaque glass of special composition, which is cast in sheets
of about 12 feet by 9 feet and from $\frac{1}{4}$ inch to $\frac{1}{2}$ inch thick.
One side of this is then polished and shows a·clean hard
surface resembling porcelain. There is a very great variety
of colouring, from white to black, both flat and streaky,
some of the variegated shades giving an effect somewhat
resembling marble, but with a different character of marking.
This stuff can be cut with the diamond much after the
fashion of plate glass, though not always with the same
ease and certainty.

The decoration of it is accomplished by means of sand-
blast and oil-painting or gilding. The design is first
worked out by means of the sand-blast, all parts which have
to appear in colour or gilding being abraded, in order to
remove the polished surface and afford a hold for the paint.
On this roughened surface oil-paint holds particularly well

FIG. 36.—Brilliant Cutting on Obscured Ground.
Designed by A. L. Duthie.

and is at least as permanent on it as elsewhere, but this is undoubtedly the weak point of the process, as the paint cannot possibly have the permanence of the glass background. The work is suitable for wall decoration, for signboards, etc. In their undecorated condition the glass plates make a splendid lining for walls, ceilings, etc., affording good colour, reflected light, and an absolutely clean, hygienic surface.

The process is of Continental origin, and some very artistic pieces of work have been executed by means of it. The freedom of design is, of course, very great, the finished effect being due very largely to the painted work.

" Vitresco " is the name given to an exceedingly ingenious process introduced and patented by the Lancashire Sand Blast Decorating Works, 9 Charles Street, Princess Street, Manchester. It may be described as a combination of fretwork and inlay, and is produced by means of the sand-blast. A fretlike design is cut out of a sheet of opal, opalescent or other opaque glass, and is then inlaid upon a base of " Marmorite," which is hollowed out to receive it, and the two are united by means of a specially prepared fireproof and waterproof cement. The effect produced is that of inlay with a small amount of relief, but this can be modified by sinking the intaglio a little deeper, and so bringing the inlaid part down to the same surface as the background. The freedom of design is practically unlimited, as the sand-blast will cut the most intricate forms with as great ease as the most simple, and the range of colour is also very wide, comprising the full range of tints in which Marmorite, opal, and opalescent glasses are made. As many colours as desired can be introduced into one design, and the surface of leaves, flowers, etc., can be marked with veins, fibres, and other lines by means of the sand-blast. Marble, stone, metal, etc., may be used for the base in place of glass with equal facility.

The cost, considering the high durability of the materials, the ease of cleaning, and the very artistic effect attainable is very reasonable, and the number of ways in which the process can be turned to account almost innumerable. For wall or ceiling decoration, for external work, on pilasters, panels, signboards, monuments, and so on, it is eminently suitable and ought to meet with a large demand. Amongst other things, it can be used for affixing letters and ornamental devices to plate-glass windows in far more secure fashion than can be attained by any other means, the rough surface produced by the sand-blast giving a much better key for the cement than the smooth surface of the polished plate.

The perforation of the fret design is managed by fixing the glass with a special elastic cement to a temporary support from which it can be easily removed when cutting is completed. The glass is then covered with a resist of blotting paper treated with glue and acids, which is cut away with a stencil knife until only that part representing the finished shape is left. It is then exposed to the sand-blast, under the action of which the uncovered glass very quickly disappears. So effective is the resist that it will withstand the blast until glass $\frac{1}{8}$ inch thick is completely eaten through. The bed in the base plate which is to receive the inlay is then hollowed out a shade larger all round than the fret which drops neatly into it and is secured by the cement.

The sand-blast has been in use for years for perforating glass for ventilators, etc., but this is the first attempt to turn perforation to artistic advantage. The process so far has hardly done more than pass the experimental stage, but all initial difficulties have been overcome, successful and beautiful work has been produced, and the prospects of a successful career for it are very bright.

One fact about it worth noting is that it offers a much more satisfactory method of decorating Marmorite slabs, than do painting and gilding, which are too foreign to the nature of the material.

A process of printing upon glass in fusible enamels is worked by Messrs. Kayll & Co., Alfred Street, Leeds. The work is mostly in the nature of advertising showcards, signs, etc., the main feature of the process being the facility for reproduction in very large numbers at a low cost, and opal is the glass most frequently employed. The printing is done from lithographic stones in an ordinary lithographic printing press. The colours employed are glass enamels, fixed by firing in a kiln, some dozen or more " stock " colours being used with very good effect. The finished work has much the appearance of lithography upon paper, with the added brilliancy, permanency and facility for cleaning which the glass affords, and ought to have a successful vogue for advertising purposes.

CHAPTER IX

THE following are descriptions of processes for glass decoration, mostly dealing with the use of hydrofluoric acid and sand-blast, for which patents have been granted. The list does not pretend to be either exhaustive or selective. Some of the processes described are almost comic in their naïveté; one or two of them are almost repetitions of some of their predecessors, but in many there are suggestions which may prove useful to workers who are seeking to extend the scope of their craft, and who require some record of what has already been done. Many of them, of course, are obsolete—have been tried and found wanting—but still they have some historical value.

EMBOSSING.

1489—1856, C. D. GARDISSAL.

This invention deals with the methods of applying the resist before acting on the uncoated portions of the glass with hydrofluoric acid. The resist is composed of a mixture of colophony and beeswax, or of elemi and Judæa bitumen, or of dammar and Judæa bitumen. The best is said to be a mixture of soft elemi with twice its weight of Judæa bitumen. The mixture is effected by fusing the two ingredients together. When set it is powdered as finely as possible.

This is used in one of the three following ways:—(1) The whole surface of the glass is rubbed over with turps. A stencil is laid on and the powder spread over it. The stencil is then lifted and takes the powder with it, except from the parts to be protected. The glass is then heated to melt the resist, which takes place without alteration of the outline. (2) The powder resist is made into a paste with soapy water and painted all over the glass. A stencil is then laid on, and all the resist not protected by the stencil is removed. The glass is then heated to melt the resist left on the glass. (3) The design is applied by means of lithographic stones, or if there are fine close lines by means of brass or steel plates. The plate is inked with a resist made by melting together 3 lb. bitumen, 3 lb. turpentine, and 2 lb. stearine. It is then scraped so as to remove all the ink except in the hollows, and an impression is taken from it on paper. The paper is then wet with very dilute hydrochloric acid and steamed over hot water to make it give up its ink more readily. The pattern is then printed off on to the glass, and when the resist is dry the hydrofluoric acid is applied.

GLASS ENGRAVING.

1002—1858, JAMES NAPIER.

Any print or design drawn by hand with printer's ink on paper is pasted down on the glass with the inked side next to the glass. When the paste is quite dry the glass is acted upon by hydrofluoric acid of about 1—14 specific gravity for three minutes. On washing then with water the acid and paper will be removed, and the glass will be left etched except where the resist was transferred to it.

Ornamenting Glass Surfaces.

1637—1858, C. Doley, E. Bigland and T. Worral, Stafford.

The pattern to be applied is first drawn upon glass with a composition of beeswax, tallow and pitch, and etched in with fluoric acid. The composition is then scraped off and the glass fastened down by means of plaster of Paris to a slate or stone slab. The etched part is filled up with a composition of beeswax, shellac, tar varnish and gas black. An impression is taken upon unsized paper, which is then damped and placed upon the article on which the pattern is to be reproduced. The printed paper is rubbed down with an indiarubber roller and afterwards washed off with warm water and soap. The article is put into a tank of dilute nitric acid. After a short time the article is removed and well washed with a strong lye made of potash, lime, soap and water. This removes all the composition, and the article will appear with the pattern sunk into the body.

Relief Effects.

2973—1860, W. T. Walter and Charles Henry.

All parts of the surface to be obtained in relief are first coated with a resist. The surface is then immersed in hydrofluoric acid.

Metal Stencil.

208—1861, Charles Bichop.

Part of the surface of the glass is protected by metal, while the rest is dulled or ground with wet sand or emery, applied by hand or by wheel brushes made of wire. The pattern may be dull on a transparent ground or transparent on a dull ground according as the metal plate protects the ground or the pattern. The process may be applied to flat or curved glass, the metal being held closely to the glass during the operation by screws or springs.

GLASS ORNAMENTING.

1981—1864, F. KUHLUNN, Paris.

The glass is ornamented by allowing solutions thickened by gum or dextrine to crystallise upon it, either all over the surface or in predetermined portions so as to form a pattern. Colouring matters may be combined with the crystalline salts *ad libitum*. The crystals being soluble in water, are covered and protected when fully formed by any colourless varnish. Vitrification in an oven may be resorted to as a means of fixing the crystals. They may also be coloured by subjecting them to chemical change before fixing. Thus, if sulphate of copper has been crystallised on the glass, exposure to sulphuretted hydrogen will convert it into black sulphide of copper without affecting the ornamental form of the crystals. Another method of colouring the crystals is to fix them with a varnish which, while transparent, is coloured with a dye or by the natural colouring matter of the resin. Hydrofluoric acid can be used, liquid or in gaseous form. The crystals will hinder the access of the acid to the glass, or the parts of the glass uncovered by crystals may be protected by a resist.

DAMASK PATTERNS.

469—1868, J. WENDEN AND S. TUSSEL, London.

In order to produce a diaper or damask pattern on the surface of glass it is first ground and the pattern laid on with varnish instead of etching it with acid. The varnish naturally clears the obscure to some extent and produces an effect resembling embossing.

OPAL AND ENAMEL IMITATIONS.

1747—1868, J. VIDIE, Pantin, Paris.

Imitations of opal and enamel can be made on glass by applying a mixture of :—

Silicate of Soda at 40°	...	...	...	300 parts.
White Enamel (powder)	...	...	...	20 ,,
Oxide of Zinc ...	...	...	...	40 ,,

After being treated with this composition the article is placed in a kiln or oven to dry. For colour designs the white enamel should be substituted by coloured enamel.

PRINTING.

1102—1870, A. A. WILBAUX.

Letters or a pattern are printed on glass by means of elastic types in a mixture of finely powdered fluor spar and viscid mass such as printing ink. Sulphuric acid is then applied to the glass with a brush or by dipping. The acid acts on the fluor spar, forming hydrofluoric acid, which etches the glass, and being kept within bounds by the printing ink, only affects the glass at the printed places.

An alternative process is to apply printing ink only by means of the types and then to flood the plate with hydrofluoric acid or to expose it to vapour of that substance. After rinsing the printing ink is removed.

Raised Patterns.

1420—1870, T. Webb, Manchester.

To obtain a raised pattern on glass dishes or vases the glass is placed in moulds. In order to secure a dim surface to the raised portion hydrochloric acid is applied, the ground portion being covered with wax in order to protect it from the action of the acid. If desired this operation may be reversed.

Original Sand-Blast Patent.

2147—1870, B. C. Tilghman.

This is the original patent by which the sand-blast was first introduced into Britain. A stream of sand is driven against the glass by means of a jet of steam, air or water, and made to act on different parts by moving the jet of sand or the surface of the glass or by moving both of them. The inventor inclines to the belief that steam is the best agent for driving the sand, as it is the easiest thing to get at high pressures. The purer and sharper the sand is the better. The use of stencils in making patterns on glass by means of the sand-blast is particularly mentioned, and indiarubber is specially stated to be the most suitable protective substance, while parchment and parchment paper, as well as the composition used for printing rollers, are spoken of as answering the purpose of shielding parts of the glass from the abrading action of the sand. The finer the sand used and the less the pressure of the blast the finer is the grain of the depolished surface, and the weaker and more delicate may be the texture of the covering substances used to produce the design.

ENGRAVING ON GLASS.

2291—1870, W. WEBB, Wordsley, Staffs.

The impressions to be engraved on the glass are first produced upon steel, copper, or stone. They are then transferred to the glass by means of suitable inks and burnt into the glass in the following manner :—A tank of gutta-percha contains a mixture of hydrofluoric acid, 50 parts, and nitric acid, 1 part. The glass is placed on a revolving shaft which rotates within the tank, and at each revolution the glass is submerged in the fluid and withdrawn. This operation is continued until the proper depth is burnt in.

SECOND SAND-BLAST PATENT.

2900—1870, B. C. TILGHMAN.

This patent is an addition to the original patent, No. 2147 of the same year, and describes methods other than those therein mentioned for driving the sand against the surface to be acted upon. Three new methods are added. One consists in driving the sand horizontally by the motion of a paddle wheel rotating rapidly in a case into the top of which the sand funnel opens. Another is to feed the sand into a vertical pipe, from which it passes by gravitation through a trunnion into a hollow axle from which proceed several pipes. The axle being set in rapid rotation, the sand escapes with great force from the orifices of the pipes. In addition to these two applications of centrifugal force, the patent protects a gravity sand-blast pure and simple, and thus anticipates Morse's patent of 1871. A very tall vertical tube is filled with sand, which escapes at the bottom from a jet which is capable of being placed at any desired angle.

GRAVITY SAND-BLAST.

2934—1871, G. F. MORSE.

A mixture of corundum and emery is placed in a finely powdered state in a hopper, the bottom of which is about 8 feet above the glass to be acted upon. A small tube from the bottom of the hopper opens just above the glass, and, by means of a sliding valve, allows the grinding mixture to fall down the tube and impinge upon the glass. A tray is provided to catch the falling material for return to the hopper from time to time after sifting.

ENGRAVING GLASS WITH BORIC ACID.

802—1873, EDOUARD DODÉ.

Boric acid is used instead of hydrofluoric. The polish is first taken off the glass by spreading very fine sand on it and rubbing with a piece of sheet iron or zinc. A boric acid composition—2,000 grammes of acid made into a paste with water and 50 grammes of gum arabic—is then applied with a brush to the parts to be etched. The glass is dried and heated in an oven to a temperature sufficient to fuse the boric acid. The composition may be coloured as desired. The parts of the glass acted on by the boric acid recover some of their original brilliance and are left semi-transparent.

EMBOSSING GLASS.

2752—1874, THADDEUS HYATT.

This seems to be one of the earliest, if not the earliest patent for embossing plate glass while it is still soft on the casting table. The accessory use of the sand-blast is mentioned in the specification.

FIXING DESIGNS ON GLASS.

5054—1875, J. MORRISON, Lanark, N.B.

The surface is coated with copal varnish and the glass placed in a stove. When the varnish is brought to a sticky condition the design is transferred to the glass from a paper impression taken from a lithographic stone or engraved plate. The glass is stoved until dry. The surface is then rubbed down with pumice stone and again coated with varnish and the glass re-stoved. When dry the surface is rubbed down, smoothed with rottenstone and polished.

LIGHT AND SHADE EFFECTS ON EMBOSSED GLASS.

3268—1876, C. HOLLYER, Walworth Road, London.

The embossed glass is first cleaned with a weak solution of sulphuric acid in water and afterwards with pure water. A combination of red lead and Brunswick black is laid on. Stencil plates are placed on this in which parts are cut expressly to form the light while other plates are placed on to form the shades of the pattern already embossed. The open parts are treated with turpentine to take out the red lead and Brunswick black, after which they are washed with milk so as to leave a film on the embossed parts and also on the ground parts. This operation retards the too rapid action of the acid, which is then applied and allowed to remain for two hours. It is then poured off and the glass washed with caustic potash diluted with water. This completes the process and leaves the glass with distinct tones of light and shade.

Fig. 37.—Example of Pearce's Patent Vitrémure.
One of several panels fixed at the Roman Catholic Church,
Stamford Hill, London.

PRINTING.

3942—1876, JOHN UNWIN.

A design or lettering is printed on the glass by means of elastic blocks, made of glue and treacle, indiarubber, or gutta-percha and inked with printing ink. The glass is then dusted over with rosin and shaken so that the rosin remains on the printed place only. The glass is then varnished at the back to keep the etching liquid from the back, and the unprinted parts of the front are matt-etched with a mixture of 2 lb. hydrofluoric acid, 2 lb. soda ash, and 24 lb. water. When the desired degree of etching has been reached, the glass is rinsed with water, then with a solution of carbonate of soda, and finally with water again.

IRIDESCENT EFFECTS.

954—1877, L. CLEMANDOT, Paris.

Glass may have an iridescent effect imparted to it by submitting it to a pressure of from 2 to 5 or 6 atmospheres. This effect may be improved if water acidulated with 15 per cent. hydrochloric acid is applied under the same pressure at a temperature of from 120° to 150° Cent. This treatment gives the glass an appearance resembling mother-of-pearl.

NOVEL METHOD OF APPLYING A RESIST.

2016—1881, S. H. CROCKER.

This rather fanciful patent protects the application of a resist on glass to be etched with hydrofluoric by the use of a pen which is kept hot during use so that the resist will flow from it. The best resist for the purpose is made by fusing together 6 lb. of rosin, 6 lb. of wax, and 2 lb. of lamp black. The pen is an ordinary steel one. The nib is heated either by a tiny gas jet connected with the gas supply by a flexible tube which does not hinder thé movements of the pen, or by a small spirit lamp attached to the pen-holder. It may also be heated by electric wires.

Avoiding Fumes.

3745—1881, Julius Fahdt.

To avoid the fumes of hydrofluoric acid, the inventor applies to the parts of the glass to be etched a thick paste of a dry fluoride mixed with gum, starch and varnish. This may be applied with a brush or rubber stamp, or the vehicle may be first applied and dry fluoride dusted over it. The mass will then absorb moisture hygroscopically from the atmosphere and gradually act corrosively upon the glass without evolving any fumes, injurious or otherwise.

Matting with Liquid Hydrofluoric.

1000—1882, W. Grune.

Liquid hydrofluoric acid applied in the usual way leaves the etched part semi-transparent. The patentee divides his invention into two processes. In the first a matted pattern is produced, and in the second a bright pattern with a matt ground. In the former case the pattern is put upon the glass by direct drawing or by transfer with an oil varnish. It is then powdered over with bronze powder and the liquid acid applied by dipping or with a brush. In a few seconds the powder scales off, and the glass is then rinsed. The action is so rapid that the bright parts require no protection with resist. According to the degree of coarseness of the powder a coarse or fine-grained matt can be produced. To get a bright pattern on a matt ground, the pattern is put upon the glass first with resist. When this is dry the whole surface is covered with the oil varnish and powdered with the bronze powder. The glass is then treated with hydrofluoric acid as above described, and when the acid has been rinsed off the resist is removed with an alkaline lye.

ORNAMENTING GLASS.

2025—1882, C. BISHOP, St. Helens, Lancs.

The object is to provide means whereby objects of glass of any shape may be easily ornamented with a device of any pattern either sunk into the surface of the glass or in relief. A printing ink composed of glue, glycerine, flour and yellow ochre is made to resist the action of the sandblast. The pattern is printed on tissue paper from a wood, metal or stone block, and then transferred to the article.

EMPLOYING ALKALIES.

2265—1883, J. KING, Liverpool.

An effect similar to that produced by etching with hydrofluoric acid can be obtained by applying a fixed alkali to the glass. The alkali is dissolved in water to which is added a little starch and applied to the glass. It is then placed in an oven and subjected to a gradually increasing temperature until the water evaporates. When this is accomplished a thin film of varnish is painted over the surface in order to prevent the deposited salt from scaling off. The heat is then gradually raised until the desired reaction between the alkali and the silica of the glass takes place. It is kept at that temperature for a few minutes and then allowed to cool gradually. It is then thoroughly washed.

Etching Glass.

2266—1883, H. Schultze, Berge.

The pattern on the glass is produced by applying solid fluorides and then firing. Two methods are employed. In one the solid fluoride is made into an ink with Venice turpentine. With this ink the pattern is drawn upon the glass. In the other a varnish is painted over the surface, and lace or other reticulated fabric previously soaked in a liquid fluoride is pressed into it while wet. In either case the glass is etched where the fluoride has come into contact with it. The temperature required is rather high—about 750° Fahr.—so that in the case of very fusible glass it is better to use a lower temperature and assist the action by exposing the surface to the fumes of boiling sulphuric.

Improvements in Glass Tablets.

3671—1894, Samuel Pollard.

This invention deals with the production of matt patterns or letters by means of French acid, made by mixing hydrofluoric acid with carbonate of ammonia in various proportions according to the degree of opacity required. The smaller the proportion of ammonia salt the fainter is the matting and the greater the transparency. The effect is greatly increased by silvering or gilding the back of the glass.

Giving Glass the Appearance of Marble.
12901—1884, J. Budd, Finchley Road, Surrey.

This invention describes a method whereby sheets of glass may be made to appear like marble, malachite or onyx. A vat is partly filled with lime in water, two parts water to one part lime. An ordinary pigment mixed with oil and of any desired colour or colours is placed in the solution, on which it will float. The glass is then placed on the floating colours, which will be transferred from the surface of the limewater to the glass. When these have dried the background can be painted on. It is then coated with a mixture of shellac and plaster of Paris, and can be used for the decoration of ceilings, etc.

Imitation Mosaic Work on Glass.
12902—1884, J. Budd.

The design to be applied is lithographed on paper and then transferred to the glass by the aid of a paste composed of nitrate of strontium and ordinary starch dissolved in water and boiled. Some of this is applied to the surface of the glass and a small quantity to the paper bearing the design. The paper is then laid on the glass and covered with a sheet of oilcloth. Pressure is applied to remove the superfluous paste which will ooze out round the edges. The glass with the pattern transferred to it is placed on a heated table and dried. The paper is rubbed with sand-paper until only a thin layer of it remains adhering to the design. The glass is again placed on the heated table, and over the remaining thin substance of paper is applied sper-maceti or paraffin wax. This imparts a lustre and brilliancy and forms a waterproof coating.

Engraving Glass.

12656—1885, Arthur Martyn.

Glass is treated with a resist consisting of copal varnish thickened by heat and dusted over with asphaltum before the varnish dries. The superfluous asphaltum having been blown away, the glass is heated until the asphaltum melts into the copal. When this compound resist is set, the glass is acted upon by liquid or gaseous hydrofluoric according to whether a bright or a matt etching is required.

Gilding Glass.

12014—1885, J. Pratt.

The surface is thoroughly cleaned and then treated with a solution of tin chloride, after which it is washed with distilled water. The glass is removed to a heated inclined table, and a solution of gold in aqua regia, mixed with pure caustic soda and glycerine, with or without mannite, is poured over till a sufficiently thick deposit is left. The gold surface is then, after washing with distilled water, silver-backed by pouring thereupon a mixture of silver nitrate, ammonia and Rochelle salts, and the metallic coatings protected by varnish or paint as usual.

Bichromate Printing.

5978—1886, F. Winterhoff.

This patent deals chiefly with bichromate printing on glass. The glass is coated with gelatine and bichromate in a dark room, and the part to be etched is covered while still soft with metal foil or powder by means of a stencil or otherwise. The plate is then exposed to light, which renders the uncovered parts of the gelatine insoluble. The metal-covered portions are then washed away with water, and after drying the glass is exposed to hydrofluoric acid.

A Novel Resist.

11551—1888, W. Lutwyche.

Sand or small shot is scattered over the glass, which is then bordered with wax and exposed to hydrofluoric.

Designs on Glass.

2358—1889, D. Reich, Vienna.

This is a combination of white acid and sand-blast. The glass is first obscured by means of white acid, and then has a pattern worked on it by means of sand-blast, which is of course somewhat more opaque than the ground.

Frosting Glass.

6446—1889, J. E. Matthewson, Sheffield.

The glass is frosted with very fine sand mixed with water to form mud. The frosting produced by using the sand in this state is much finer than that obtained by the old method of using dry sand. Moreover, the action is quicker, and there is no dust, while the mud can be easily collected for use again. The mud is projected against the glass by a jet of steam, air or gas under considerable pressure.

Etching Liquids.

12155—1890, B. Z. Meth and Kreitner.

Glass is etched by means of a liquid applied by a rubber stamp. The liquid is prepared in two separate portions, A and B.

A consists of—

Ammonium fluoride	...	...	40 oz.
Common salt	...	...	..	2 oz.
Carbonate of soda ...	...	...	2 oz.
Concentrated sulphuric acid	...	8 oz.
Fuming hydrofluoric acid ...	...	16 oz.

B consists of—

Crystal potassium fluoride	...	2 oz.
Hydrofluoric acid	...	...	...	4 oz.

Solution B is made by the aid of heat, and both solutions are made in leaden vessels. They are mixed for use with the addition of a little ammonia and water glass.

MARKING GLASS.

1974—1892, WILLIAM LEADER.

The following is the entire specification of this patent, omitting the preamble and the claim : " By steeping brown paper stencils in hydrofluoric acid and pressing on the articles to be decorated with heated silver sand." This is a model of, at least, brevity.

A SILKY BACKGROUND.

15341—1893, A. S. AND W. GIBBS, Blackfriars Road, S.E.

In order to give shaded embossing with a clear bright outline we first coat the glass completely with an acid resist. The resist is then removed from the parts forming the background to the desired design by aid of a stencil. Over the surface is poured a solution of soda and fluoric acid. This has the effect of laying a white matt on all the unprotected parts. The solution is then removed, and the glass is allowed to dry. The scum left by the solution is brushed away, pure fluoric acid is poured over the surface and allowed to remain until it has etched to a sufficient depth to produce a rich silky white; the resist is then removed with mineral oil and the glass thoroughly cleaned.

A coat of stain is then laid over the surface, and with the aid of a steel straight edge is removed from the ornament, but left in the etched background. The glass is then placed in a kiln in order that the stain may be burnt in. After passing through the kiln the outline is traced on the clean glass, and the background is filled in with acid resist. A solution of soda and hydrofluoric acid is then again poured on the glass, and this forms a white matt on all the unprotected parts, leaving the outline clear, as it is protected by the resist.

If it is desired to produce out of stain a shaded embossing with clear stain outline, the glass leaving the kiln as above described is marked with the outline, the ornament to be left in clear stain, with embossing black or any usual acid resist. The white matt is then made with French acid; the glass is dried, brushed, and treated with fluoric acid again to bring out the ornament.

SPECIALLY SHARP ETCHING.
20533—1893, J. RETZLAFF.

It is claimed that the process here patented gives etchings distinguished by special sharpness of the contours and exact reproduction of the pattern, and that it is specially adapted to the manufacture of large quantities. A layer of tinfoil is cemented to the glass with an asphalt varnish. A pattern is then printed or stencilled on the tinfoil with grease colours. The bare portions of the tinfoil are then etched away with acid, and the asphalt under them is removed. The glass thus laid bare is then treated with hydrofluoric.

IMITATION EMBOSSED GLASS.

4776—1895, F. GRIFFIN, East Moulsey, Surrey.

The design is painted on the glass with a copal varnish. If the surface, when dry, is uneven or glossy, it may be rubbed down with a pad supplied with ground glass, pumice or rouge.

IMPROVED SAND-BLAST.

991—1896, T. TRUCHELUT.

In this invention the sand-blast is mixed with a chemical capable of assisting its action. Thus in the case of glass the sand is wetted with hydrofluoric acid, and the wet sand is driven against the glass to be etched.

SURFACE GROUNDS FOR EMBOSSED GLASS.

12682—1897, T. T. JONES AND H. FERMIN.

This invention is concerned with the production of a variegated surface showing a number of small matted spots or streaks interspersed with bright portions. The Brunswick black is dabbed over the surface with a sponge or feather or a crumpled piece of paper. The use of small shot is also mentioned.

VITREOUS DECORATION OF PANELS OR WALLS WITH GLASS.

21146—1897, W. J. PEARCE, LTD., 12 & 14, Albert St., Manchester.

A design first made upon paper is cut out of sheets of plain or coloured glass. Each piece of glass is cut as large as the exigencies of the design will permit. The rough side of the glass is used to produce the front of the finished decoration. If any of the pieces of glass require to be coloured, they are then stained, and any required lines or shading may be added. This treatment must be applied to the smooth side of the glass, *i.e.*, to the back of the decoration. In this way the lustrous surface, so objectionable in work of this kind, is entirely avoided, while a smooth mirror-like surface can of course be produced if desired by reversing the process. Gold or other metals can be applied as readily as colour. The glass is then fixed in position upon the wall by means of a putty-like cement.

Transferring Designs on Glass.

23080—1897, W. S. Hadley, F. W. Sephton and R. Mills.

Designs are transferred in fatty ink from etched glass plates to the surfaces, and serve as resists for etching, sandblast, silvering, or are burnt on. To prepare the etched plate, a plane surface of plate glass is coated with metal foil, wax, asphaltum or other resistant material, and a design cut in this. The design is bitten in with hydrofluoric acid, and afterwards treated with commercial ammonium fluoride or sand-blast to produce a suitable surface; the resistant material is then cleaned off. To obtain a transfer the plate is sponged with glycerine, water or oil, and covered with ink consisting of equal parts of beeswax and commercial pitch, with metallic oxides or other colouring matter; this is warmed and poured on the plate, and the excess is removed with a warmed scraper. A print is taken off, preferably on waxed paper, and transferred by rubbing or pressure to the surface to be ornamented, which is then etched with acid, sand-blasted, silvered or fired.

ENAMELLED GLASS TILES.

4220—1898, J. J. KAYLL.

Coloured enamels are painted on the smooth, ground or sand-blasted backs of opal glass facing-tiles, and fixed by firing in a glass kiln. These tiles are arranged to form designs of figure work, etc., and cemented to walls.

GRAINING GLASS.

9337—1898, HAAS & Co.

To get a very fine grain on glass, a mixture of dragon's blood and asphalt, both in powder, is stirred up in a close chamber. The coarse dust settles again, but the finest part ascends through a vertical shaft into a second chamber, where it settles on the glass plate. In this way the plate is uniformly dusted over with minute particles in very close proximity to one another. The plate is then gently heated and exposed to the vapour of hydrofluoric acid. The warmth prevents any condensation of acid, so that none of it gets under the particles of powder, and the plate is thus etched with a very fine grain, and is suitable for making screens for photographic purposes.

ETCHING GLASS.

22698—1898, H. H. MAY.

The pattern is cut in relief or intaglio on a wooden block. An impression is then taken in tinfoil, the raised portions of which are coated with a resist, and it is applied to the glass to which the adhesive cements it. The tinfoil is then etched, and the exposed adhesive is removed from the glass with turpentine. The glass laid bare is then etched with hydrofluoric.

EMBOSSING GLASS WITH SHADED DESIGNS.
19706—1899, S. JONES.

The design or lettering is drawn on the glass with a resist. When the black is dry the plate is etched with one part of hydrofluoric to five of water for about twenty minutes. After rinsing and drying, those parts of the letters which are not to be matted are blacked. The plate is then treated with white acid.

ETCHING ON ENAMEL COATING.
14105—1900, KARL TELINCK.

If glass is coated with a fusible enamel and the enamel engraved it will become covered with various thicknesses of enamel. The hydrofluoric is then employed, the acid penetrating the thinner parts of the enamel more than the thicker parts, and hence etching the glass more deeply at those points. The engraving on the enamel will be transferred to the glass as an exact copy.

COATING GLASS WITH METALS.
430—1901, R. LANGHANS.

Glass can be coated with precious metals such as gold, platinum and iridium or mixtures of these by the use of compounds of such metals or their halogen salts with sulphur derivatives of aliphatic carbon compounds; alkyl sulphides, mercaptans, sulphines, thio-aldehydes, mercaptals, thio-ketones, and mercaptols are mentioned. The compound is dissolved in bromoform, chloroform, alcohol, a volatile hydrocarbon or volatile solvent, and the glass coated with the solution.   The solvent is then evaporated and the glass warmed till the compound melts, then further heated till it decomposes, bright coherent metal being produced.   A compound of platinic chloride or proto-chloride with ethyl sulphide is preferred.

Photo Engraving Upon Glass.

26365—1901.   Jean Bossan.

A negative having been obtained upon a sensitised plate or film, it is applied to the glass, previously coated with bichromate and gelatine.   After exposure to light, the glass is coated with oil or ordinary printer's ink.   The sensitised gelatine is now developed in water, and then dusted over with a resist such as colophony or Judæa bitumen, which adheres to the greasy preserved portions.   The surface thus prepared is heated to 100 or 150 degrees C., whereby the resist is amalgamated with the emulsion and a strong protective layer formed.   The etching then proceeds in the usual way.

Glass Tiles.

14085—1903.   A. Schuber.

Glass tiles for staircases, bath walls, sign-boards, mosaics, etc., are made by fusing sheets of precious metal on the back of glass plates which may have been previously decorated and then covering this metal with cement such as water-glass cement and quartz powder.   This plate is secured to a backing such as asbestos cement.   If the plates are to be kept for some time before use the cement whilst wet is

FIG. 38.—Example of Electro-Copper Glazing.

dusted over with sand and when dry is coated with oil paint or the like.

ORNAMENTAL ENAMELLED GLASS.

22250—1903. S. JONES AND A. COURT.

This patent relates to the production of ornamented enamelled glass tablets and plates for shop fronts, door panels, swing signs, windows, pilasters, advertising, etc. A picture or design is embossed or incised on the plate by acid, a cutting tool, sand-blast or other means, and transparent or opaque pigments with gold if required are applied and fixed by firing. The painting and firing operations may be repeated several times. With opaque colours a plain polished sheet of plate glass may be used.

LITHOGRAPHIC PICTURES ON GLASS.

20904—1904. W. SCHELL, Offenburg, Baden.

The glass plate is coated on one side with a spirit varnish or black japan. When this is dry a positive or negative lithographic impression is taken upon it. As much of the varnish as is not protected by the lithographic ink is then dissolved off and the glass etched with hydrofluoric.

The glass may be first coated with gold or silver leaf instead of with varnish. In this case the metal left after printing is removed with a brush or by means of acid.

FROSTED PATTERNS.

27591—1904. O. C. HAWKES, Birmingham.

Patterns on glass are obtained by frosting by means of grinding or sand-blasting parts of the surface. The remainder is protected by a stencil. Channels are also cut in the glass by the sand-blast or by rolling and filled with coloured glass or enamel.

ORNAMENTING GLASS.

8477—1905. P. J. HANDEL.

In this process a coating of vitrifiable colour is first applied to the surface of the glass; and upon this becoming dry and hard a coating of glue, etc., is applied. The glass is then baked at a moderate temperature, causing the glue to crack, carrying away with it parts of the colour beneath it together with flakes of the glass. The surface acquires a tint from the colour, which may be removed, if desired, by the use of hydrofluoric acid.

BEVELLED PLATE GLASS.

8819—1905, PRESSED PRISM PLATE GLASS Co., Morgan Town, U.S.A.

This method dispenses with the necessity of grinding and polishing in order to produce a bevelled edge to plate glass. The glass sheet is distributed in process of manufacture upon a table by means of a roller which has angular projections arranged in rectangular or other outline depending on the size and shape of the plates to be produced. After passing beneath the roller the table with the glass sheet upon it is carried beneath a pressing die bearing projections exactly similar to those on the roller. The action of the die is to finish the grooves partly formed by the roller. When this operation is complete the glass is divided along the lines of the base of the grooves formed by the roller and die. The margins of the pieces so divided will have properly bevelled edges. It is evident that the process can only be employed when a large number of plates is required to one size or shape.

MARBLED GLASS.
15452—1905, F. W. BUNDY.

Marbled effects can be produced on glass by covering the surface with a vitrifiable colouring substance in the form of powder, applying a flexible waterproof surface, previously splashed with a solution of gummy substances in water, spirit or other volatile liquid, removing the waterproof covering and allowing the irregularly wetted surface to dry. The surface is then dusted with a fine camel-hair brush and the process repeated with other colouring substances. The work is fixed by firing in a kiln.

AUTOMATIC MACHINE FOR BEVELLING PLATE GLASS.
1047—1906, J. FRANKINET-KIRBY, 336, Rue des Goujons, Brussels.

The work table is adjusted laterally relatively to a support behind it by means of a screw spindle. The support bears solely upon a single guide rail which is of a circular iron section. The back of the table, which is provided with a rubber seating in place of the usual wooden one, bears against guide rollers. By rotating a nut on the screw spindle the degree of inclination of the table is regulated.

GLASS POLISHING MACHINE.
2132—1906, H. A. WALDRICH, Siegen, Germany.

In this machine the polishing felt is simply secured to the shoe of the polishing block. The shoe is fixed to the block by means of dovetail joints, tenons or screws. This obviates the necessity of unscrewing the whole block with the spindle, hand-wheel spring and bracket whenever the felt has to be changed, an operation hitherto necessary owing to the construction of the shoe.

Mills for Bevelling Glass.

13612—1906, W. O. Bailey, Wenlock Road, City Road, London, N.

A pair of mills are mounted so that their axes are not parallel with each other. The amount of angularity is governed by the amount of set-off on the mill face. For this purpose the mills are arranged so that their up-cut sides are adjacent. The mills are provided with protecting rings and fed with a polishing medium by means of a pulsating feeding device. The advantages of the contrivance are that the cutting effect is greatly improved and a smaller amount of polishing medium need be used.

Glass Bevelling Machine.

15504—1906, G. L. Goehring, Akron, Ohio, U.S.A.

This machine has a rotary grinder in connection with the glass support which is angularly adjustable in a frame. The frame is angularly movable and bodily adjustable to effect the proper movement and adjustment of the glass to the grinder. The machine also has mechanism whereby the grinding operation may be effected on the top portion of the grinder by a sequence of movements so that the entry of grit between the grinder and surface is avoided. By rotation of the grinder a body of water is automatically applied to the glass and grinder at the grinding point sufficient to keep the leading edge of the glass submerged.

POLISHING GLASS BEVELS.

16828—1906, H. LOHMANN, 109, Lütticherstrasse, Aix-la-Chapelle, Prussia.

In this machine the polishing heads execute one oscillating movement around their axes during the time they carry out a series of linear back and forth motions. By the use of this contrivance no unpolished spots are left on the surface, and the operation of polishing takes about half the time hitherto necessary.

GLOSSARY

—————◆—————

ANNEALING.—A prolonged and very gradual cooling to which all glass is subjected in process of manufacture to obviate risk of spontaneous breakage.

ANTIQUE GLASS.—Glass made in imitation of the colour and quality of old glass by the same methods of hand work.

BRILLIANT CUTTING.—A process of cutting or engraving upon a stone wheel used for decorating plate glass.

BEVELLING.—A process similar to above applied to the *edges* of plate glass.

CALMS.—The lead frames used in leaded lights, H-shaped in section.

CARTOON.—A working drawing made to the actual size of the work and showing all details.

CRISSLES.—Small, sometimes almost invisible, cracks, occurring generally in variegated antique glasses, and caused by imperfect annealing. They frequently cause breakage.

CULLETT.—Broken glass and waste in cutting. It is generally used up as an ingredient in the making of new glass by mixing in a larger or smaller proportion with the new materials.

CUT-LINE DRAWING.—A drawing showing only the heart of the lead—the *cutting* line—which is used in cutting and glazing leaded lights.

DOUBLING OR DOUBLE GLAZING.—The introduction of two thicknesses of glass into one lead for the purpose of modifying colour, or to obviate the necessity of firing glass which will not stand the heat of the kiln without changing colour.

EMBOSSING.—A process of etching glass by means of acids.

ENAMELS.—Pigments applied to the surface of the glass by firing but not entering into the body of it.

ENGRAVING.—*See* Brilliant Cutting.

FLANGES.—Those parts of lead calms which lie flat upon the surface of the glass.

FLASHED GLASS.—Glass having a white or pale-coloured body with a thin veneer of a stronger colour laid upon one side of it. This veneer is capable of being removed by acid or by abrasion.

FLUORIC ACID.—*See* Hydrofluoric Acid.

FLUX.—A highly fusible glass in powder form which is mixed with metallic oxides to make pigments for painting upon glass.

FLUX.—Greasy or resinous materials used in soldering to cause the solder to flow more easily, to bring it into more intimate contact with the lead and to remove dirt from the joint.

FRENCH CHALK.—A material prepared from powdered talc which is capable of marking on smooth glass surfaces.

FRENCH EMBOSSING.—A system of etching with two or more acids which seems to have originated in France.

GAUGE.—Hand and bench gauges used in cutting glass for leaded lights.

GRISAILLE.—A style of painted glass work peculiar to the thirteenth century, in which the background of the ornament was covered with a cross-hatching of narrow painted lines, producing a grey effect.

GROZING.—Biting away small fragments from the edge of a piece of glass with a pair of pliers.

HEART.—The centre of a lead calm connecting the two flanges.

LATHYKIN OR LARRIKIN.—A wooden tool used for opening flanges of lead calms.

LIGHT.—A term applied to the separate openings between the mullions of a window and, in the case of leaded lights, to the glass with which they are filled.

MULLER.—An implement of glass or granite used for grinding colour.

OBSCURE.—A term applied to glass which has been rendered non-transparent by grinding, sand-blast or acid.

PLATING.—A system of adding pieces of glass on the surface of leaded lights to modify colour.

POT METAL.—Glass which is coloured throughout its substance, as distinguished from flashed glass, which is only coloured on one side.

QUARRIES.—Diamond-shaped pieces of glass used in plain glazing. The word is derived from *quarrel*, meaning a cross-bow bolt, the head of which was lozenge-shaped.

Occasionally applied to square and oblong shapes also.

RESISTS.—Greasy or resinous substances used to resist the action of acids in etching.

SADDLE BARS.—Bars of iron, steel or brass used to strengthen leaded lights.

SAND-BLAST.—A process of abrading glass by means of sharp sand driven by a jet of steam or air.

SIGHT SIZE.—Measurements taken between the actual edges of mullions and sashes, making no allowance for the glass or lead which is hidden by the rebate or groove.

STAIN.—A preparation of silver which imparts a yellow stain to glass—the only pigment which can be applied after the glass is made which really affects its colour.

STENCIL.—A perforated sheet of paper, metal or other material used in the repetition of patterns.

STOPPING KNIFE.—A tool used in the manipulation of the lead in making and especially in repairing leaded lights.

TEMPLATES.—Patterns cut in paper, cardboard, wood, etc., to show correct shape of tracing pieces and curved heads of windows.

TESSERÆ.—Small cubes of glass used in mosaic work.

TINNING.—Coating copper, iron or other metals with tin to permit of their being soldered.

VEHICLES.—Oils, spirits, etc., used in the mixing of paints.

VICE.—Machine or mill used in converting lead calms to various sizes and sections.

INDEX

◆

A CATALOGUE OF
SELECTED DOVER BOOKS
IN ALL FIELDS OF INTEREST

A CATALOG OF SELECTED DOVER BOOKS IN ALL FIELDS OF INTEREST

LASERS AND HOLOGRAPHY, Winston E. Kock. Sound introduction to burgeoning field, expanded (1981) for second edition. 84 illustrations. 160pp. 5⅜ × 8¼. (EUK) 24041-X Pa. $3.50

FLORAL STAINED GLASS PATTERN BOOK, Ed Sibbett, Jr. 96 exquisite floral patterns—irises, poppie, lilies, tulips, geometrics, abstracts, etc.—adaptable to innumerable stained glass projects. 64pp. 8¼ × 11. 24259-5 Pa. $3.50

THE HISTORY OF THE LEWIS AND CLARK EXPEDITION, Meriwether Lewis and William Clark. Edited by Eliott Coues. Great classic edition of Lewis and Clark's day-by-day journals. Complete 1893 edition, edited by Eliott Coues from Biddle's authorized 1814 history. 1508pp. 5⅜ × 8½.
21268-8, 21269-6, 21270-X Pa. Three-vol. set $22.50

ORLEY FARM, Anthony Trollope. Three-dimensional tale of great criminal case. Original Millais illustrations illuminate marvelous panorama of Victorian society. Plot was author's favorite. 736pp. 5⅜ × 8½. 24181-5 Pa. $8.95

THE CLAVERINGS, Anthony Trollope. Major novel, chronicling aspects of British Victorian society, personalities. 16 plates by M. Edwards; first reprint of full text. 412pp. 5⅜ × 8½. 23464-9 Pa. $6.00

EINSTEIN'S THEORY OF RELATIVITY, Max Born. Finest semi-technical account; much explanation of ideas and math not readily available elsewhere on this level. 376pp. 5⅜ × 8½. 60769-0 Pa. $5.00

COMPUTABILITY AND UNSOLVABILITY, Martin Davis. Classic graduate-level introduction th theory of computability, usually referred to as theory of recurrent functions. New preface and appendix. 288pp. 5⅜ × 8½. 61471-9 Pa. $6.50

THE GODS OF THE EGYPTIANS, E.A. Wallis Budge. Never excelled for richness, fullness: all gods, goddesses, demons. mythical figures of Ancient Egypt; their legends, rites, incarnations, etc. Over 225 illustrations, plus 6 color plates. 988pp. 6⅛ × 9¼. (EBE) 22055-9, 22056-7 Pa., Two-vol. set $20.00

THE I CHING (THE BOOK OF CHANGES), translated by James Legge. Most penetrating divination manual ever prepared. Indispensable to study of early Oriental civilizations, to modern inquiring reader. 448pp. 5⅜ × 8½.
21062-6 Pa. $6.50

THE CRAFTSMAN'S HANDBOOK, Cennino Cennini. 15th-century handbook, school of Giotto, explains applying gold, silver leaf; gesso; fresco painting, grinding pigments, etc. 142pp. 6⅛ × 9¼. 20054-X Pa. $3.50

AN ATLAS OF ANATOMY FOR ARTISTS, Fritz Schider. Finest text, working book. Full text, plus anatomical illustrations; plates by great artists showing anatomy. 593 illustrations. 192pp. 7⅛ × 10¼. 20241-0 Pa. $6.00

EASY-TO-MAKE STAINED GLASS LIGHTCATCHERS, Ed Sibbett, Jr. 67 designs for most enjoyable ornaments: fruits, birds, teddy bears, trumpet, etc. Full size templates. 64pp. 8¼ × 11. 24081-9 Pa. $3.95

TRIAD OPTICAL ILLUSIONS AND HOW TO DESIGN THEM, Harry Turner. Triad explained in 32 pages of text, with 32 pages of Escher-like patterns on coloring stock. 92 figures. 32 plates. 64pp. 8¼ × 11. 23549-1 Pa. $2.50

THE MURDER BOOK OF J.G. REEDER, Edgar Wallace. Eight suspenseful stories by bestselling mystery writer of 20s and 30s. Features the donnish Mr. J.G. Reeder of Public Prosecutor's Office. 128pp. 5⅜ × 8½. (Available in U.S. only)
24374-5 Pa. $3.50

ANNE ORR'S CHARTED DESIGNS, Anne Orr. Best designs by premier needlework designer, all on charts: flowers, borders, birds, children, alphabets, etc. Over 100 charts, 10 in color. Total of 40pp. 8¼ × 11.
23704-4 Pa. $2.25

BASIC CONSTRUCTION TECHNIQUES FOR HOUSES AND SMALL BUILDINGS SIMPLY EXPLAINED, U.S. Bureau of Naval Personnel. Grading, masonry, woodworking, floor and wall framing, roof framing, plastering, tile setting, much more. Over 675 illustrations. 568pp. 6½ × 9¼.
20242-9 Pa. $8.95

MATISSE LINE DRAWINGS AND PRINTS, Henri Matisse. Representative collection of female nudes, faces, still lifes, experimental works, etc., from 1898 to 1948. 50 illustrations. 48pp. 8⅜ × 11¼.
23877-6 Pa. $2.50

HOW TO PLAY THE CHESS OPENINGS, Eugene Znosko-Borovsky. Clear, profound examinations of just what each opening is intended to do and how opponent can counter. Many sample games. 147pp. 5⅜ × 8½.
22795-2 Pa. $2.95

DUPLICATE BRIDGE, Alfred Sheinwold. Clear, thorough, easily followed account: rules, etiquette, scoring, strategy, bidding; Goren's point-count system, Blackwood and Gerber conventions, etc. 158pp. 5⅜ × 8½.
22741-3 Pa. $3.00

SARGENT PORTRAIT DRAWINGS, J.S. Sargent. Collection of 42 portraits reveals technical skill and intuitive eye of noted American portrait painter, John Singer Sargent. 48pp. 8¼ × 11⅛.
24524-1 Pa. $2.95

ENTERTAINING SCIENCE EXPERIMENTS WITH EVERYDAY OBJECTS, Martin Gardner. Over 100 experiments for youngsters. Will amuse, astonish, teach, and entertain. Over 100 illustrations. 127pp. 5⅜ × 8½.
24201-3 Pa. $2.50

TEDDY BEAR PAPER DOLLS IN FULL COLOR: A Family of Four Bears and Their Costumes, Crystal Collins. A family of four Teddy Bear paper dolls and nearly 60 cut-out costumes. Full color, printed one side only. 32pp. 9¼ × 12¼.
24550-0 Pa. $3.50

NEW CALLIGRAPHIC ORNAMENTS AND FLOURISHES, Arthur Baker. Unusual, multi-useable material: arrows, pointing hands, brackets and frames, ovals, swirls, birds, etc. Nearly 700 illustrations. 80pp. 8⅜ × 11¼.
24095-9 Pa. $3.50

DINOSAUR DIORAMAS TO CUT & ASSEMBLE, M. Kalmenoff. Two complete three-dimensional scenes in full color, with 31 cut-out animals and plants. Excellent educational toy for youngsters. Instructions; 2 assembly diagrams. 32pp. 9¼ × 12¼.
24541-1 Pa. $3.95

SILHOUETTES: A PICTORIAL ARCHIVE OF VARIED ILLUSTRATIONS, edited by Carol Belanger Grafton. Over 600 silhouettes from the 18th to 20th centuries. Profiles and full figures of men, women, children, birds, animals, groups and scenes, nature, ships, an alphabet. 144pp. 8⅜ × 11¼.
23781-8 Pa. $4.50

25 KITES THAT FLY, Leslie Hunt. Full, easy-to-follow instructions for kites made from inexpensive materials. Many novelties. 70 illustrations. 110pp. 5⅜ × 8½.
22550-X Pa. $1.95

PIANO TUNING, J. Cree Fischer. Clearest, best book for beginner, amateur. Simple repairs, raising dropped notes, tuning by easy method of flattened fifths. No previous skills needed. 4 illustrations. 201pp. 5⅜ × 8½.
23267-0 Pa. $3.50

EARLY AMERICAN IRON-ON TRANSFER PATTERNS, edited by Rita Weiss. 75 designs, borders, alphabets, from traditional American sources. 48pp. 8¼ × 11.
23162-3 Pa. $1.95

CROCHETING EDGINGS, edited by Rita Weiss. Over 100 of the best designs for these lovely trims for a host of household items. Complete instructions, illustrations. 48pp. 8¼ × 11.
24031-2 Pa. $2.00

FINGER PLAYS FOR NURSERY AND KINDERGARTEN, Emilie Poulsson. 18 finger plays with music (voice and piano); entertaining, instructive. Counting, nature lore, etc. Victorian classic. 53 illustrations. 80pp. 6½ × 9¼. 22588-7 Pa. $1.95

BOSTON THEN AND NOW, Peter Vanderwarker. Here in 59 side-by-side views are photographic documentations of the city's past and present. 119 photographs. Full captions. 122pp. 8¼ × 11.
24312-5 Pa. $6.95

CROCHETING BEDSPREADS, edited by Rita Weiss. 22 patterns, originally published in three instruction books 1939-41. 39 photos, 8 charts. Instructions. 48pp. 8¼ × 11.
23610-2 Pa. $2.00

HAWTHORNE ON PAINTING, Charles W. Hawthorne. Collected from notes taken by students at famous Cape Cod School; hundreds of direct, personal *apercus*, ideas, suggestions. 91pp. 5⅜ × 8½.
20653-X Pa. $2.50

THERMODYNAMICS, Enrico Fermi. A classic of modern science. Clear, organized treatment of systems, first and second laws, entropy, thermodynamic potentials, etc. Calculus required. 160pp. 5⅜ × 8½.
60361-X Pa. $4.00

TEN BOOKS ON ARCHITECTURE, Vitruvius. The most important book ever written on architecture. Early Roman aesthetics, technology, classical orders, site selection, all other aspects. Morgan translation. 331pp. 5⅜ × 8½. 20645-9 Pa. $5.50

THE CORNELL BREAD BOOK, Clive M. McCay and Jeanette B. McCay. Famed high-protein recipe incorporated into breads, rolls, buns, coffee cakes, pizza, pie crusts, more. Nearly 50 illustrations. 48pp. 8¼ × 11.
23995-0 Pa. $2.00

THE CRAFTSMAN'S HANDBOOK, Cennino Cennini. 15th-century handbook, school of Giotto, explains applying gold, silver leaf; gesso; fresco painting, grinding pigments, etc. 142pp. 6⅛ × 9¼.
20054-X Pa. $3.50

FRANK LLOYD WRIGHT'S FALLINGWATER, Donald Hoffmann. Full story of Wright's masterwork at Bear Run, Pa. 100 photographs of site, construction, and details of completed structure. 112pp. 9¼ × 10.
23671-4 Pa. $6.50

OVAL STAINED GLASS PATTERN BOOK, C. Eaton. 60 new designs framed in shape of an oval. Greater complexity, challenge with sinuous cats, birds, mandalas framed in antique shape. 64pp. 8¼ × 11.
24519-5 Pa. $3.50

SURREAL STICKERS AND UNREAL STAMPS, William Rowe. 224 haunting, hilarious stamps on gummed, perforated stock, with images of elephants, geisha girls, George Washington, etc. 16pp. one side. 8¼ × 11. 24371-0 Pa. $3.50

GOURMET KITCHEN LABELS, Ed Sibbett, Jr. 112 full-color labels (4 copies each of 28 designs). Fruit, bread, other culinary motifs. Gummed and perforated. 16pp. 8¼ × 11. 24087-8 Pa. $2.95

PATTERNS AND INSTRUCTIONS FOR CARVING AUTHENTIC BIRDS, H.D. Green. Detailed instructions, 27 diagrams, 85 photographs for carving 15 species of birds so life-like, they'll seem ready to fly! 8¼ × 11. 24222-6 Pa. $2.75

FLATLAND, E.A. Abbott. Science-fiction classic explores life of 2-D being in 3-D world. 16 illustrations. 103pp. 5⅜ × 8. 20001-9 Pa. $2.00

DRIED FLOWERS, Sarah Whitlock and Martha Rankin. Concise, clear, practical guide to dehydration, glycerinizing, pressing plant material, and more. Covers use of silica gel. 12 drawings. 32pp. 5⅜ × 8½. 21802-3 Pa. $1.00

EASY-TO-MAKE CANDLES, Gary V. Guy. Learn how easy it is to make all kinds of decorative candles. Step-by-step instructions. 82 illustrations. 48pp. 8¼ × 11. 23881-4 Pa. $2.50

SUPER STICKERS FOR KIDS, Carolyn Bracken. 128 gummed and perforated full-color stickers: GIRL WANTED, KEEP OUT, BORED OF EDUCATION, X-RATED, COMBAT ZONE, many others. 16pp. 8¼ × 11. 24092-4 Pa. $2.50

CUT AND COLOR PAPER MASKS, Michael Grater. Clowns, animals, funny faces...simply color them in, cut them out, and put them together, and you have 9 paper masks to play with and enjoy. 32pp. 8¼ × 11. 23171-2 Pa. $2.25

A CHRISTMAS CAROL: THE ORIGINAL MANUSCRIPT, Charles Dickens. Clear facsimile of Dickens manuscript, on facing pages with final printed text. 8 illustrations by John Leech, 4 in color on covers. 144pp. 8⅜ × 11¼. 20980-6 Pa. $5.95

CARVING SHOREBIRDS, Harry V. Shourds & Anthony Hillman. 16 full-size patterns (all double-page spreads) for 19 North American shorebirds with step-by-step instructions. 72pp. 9¼ × 12¼. 24287-0 Pa. $4.95

THE GENTLE ART OF MATHEMATICS, Dan Pedoe. Mathematical games, probability, the question of infinity, topology, how the laws of algebra work, problems of irrational numbers, and more. 42 figures. 143pp. 5⅜ × 8½. (EBE) 22949-1 Pa. $3.00

READY-TO-USE DOLLHOUSE WALLPAPER, Katzenbach & Warren, Inc. Stripe, 2 floral stripes, 2 allover florals, polka dot; all in full color. 4 sheets (350 sq. in.) of each, enough for average room. 48pp. 8¼ × 11. 23495-9 Pa. $2.95

MINIATURE IRON-ON TRANSFER PATTERNS FOR DOLLHOUSES, DOLLS, AND SMALL PROJECTS, Rita Weiss and Frank Fontana. Over 100 miniature patterns: rugs, bedspreads, quilts, chair seats, etc. In standard dollhouse size. 48pp. 8¼ × 11. 23741-9 Pa. $1.95

THE DINOSAUR COLORING BOOK, Anthony Rao. 45 renderings of dinosaurs, fossil birds, turtles, other creatures of Mesozoic Era. Scientifically accurate. Captions. 48pp. 8¼ × 11. 24022-3 Pa. $2.25

THE BOOK OF WOOD CARVING, Charles Marshall Sayers. Still finest book for beginning student. Fundamentals, technique; gives 34 designs, over 34 projects for panels, bookends, mirrors, etc. 33 photos. 118pp. 7¾ × 10⅝. 23654-4 Pa. $3.95

CARVING COUNTRY CHARACTERS, Bill Higginbotham. Expert advice for beginning, advanced carvers on materials, techniques for creating 18 projects—mirthful panorama of American characters. 105 illustrations. 80pp. 8⅜ × 11. 24135-1 Pa. $2.50

300 ART NOUVEAU DESIGNS AND MOTIFS IN FULL COLOR, C.B. Grafton. 44 full-page plates display swirling lines and muted colors typical of Art Nouveau. Borders, frames, panels, cartouches, dingbats, etc. 48pp. 9⅜ × 12¼. 24354-0 Pa. $6.00

SELF-WORKING CARD TRICKS, Karl Fulves. Editor of *Pallbearer* offers 72 tricks that work automatically through nature of card deck. No sleight of hand needed. Often spectacular. 42 illustrations. 113pp. 5⅜ × 8½. 23334-0 Pa. $2.25

CUT AND ASSEMBLE A WESTERN FRONTIER TOWN, Edmund V. Gillon, Jr. Ten authentic full-color buildings on heavy cardboard stock in H-O scale. Sheriff's Office and Jail, Saloon, Wells Fargo, Opera House, others. 48pp. 9¼ × 12¼. 23736-2 Pa. $3.95

CUT AND ASSEMBLE AN EARLY NEW ENGLAND VILLAGE, Edmund V. Gillon, Jr. Printed in full color on heavy cardboard stock. 12 authentic buildings in H-O scale: Adams home in Quincy, Mass., Oliver Wight house in Sturbridge, smithy, store, church, others. 48pp. 9¼ × 12¼. 23536-X Pa. $3.95

THE TALE OF TWO BAD MICE, Beatrix Potter. Tom Thumb and Hunca Munca squeeze out of their hole and go exploring. 27 full-color Potter illustrations. 59pp. 4¼ × 5½. (Available in U.S. only) 23065-1 Pa. $1.50

CARVING FIGURE CARICATURES IN THE OZARK STYLE, Harold L. Enlow. Instructions and illustrations for ten delightful projects, plus general carving instructions. 22 drawings and 47 photographs altogether. 39pp. 8⅜ × 11. 23151-8 Pa. $2.50

A TREASURY OF FLOWER DESIGNS FOR ARTISTS, EMBROIDERERS AND CRAFTSMEN, Susan Gaber. 100 garden favorites lushly rendered by artist for artists, craftsmen, needleworkers. Many form frames, borders. 80pp. 8¼ × 11. 24096-7 Pa. $3.50

CUT & ASSEMBLE A TOY THEATER/THE NUTCRACKER BALLET, Tom Tierney. Model of a complete, full-color production of Tchaikovsky's classic. 6 backdrops, dozens of characters, familiar dance sequences. 32pp. 9⅜ × 12¼. 24194-7 Pa. $4.50

ANIMALS: 1,419 COPYRIGHT-FREE ILLUSTRATIONS OF MAMMALS, BIRDS, FISH, INSECTS, ETC., edited by Jim Harter. Clear wood engravings present, in extremely lifelike poses, over 1,000 species of animals. 284pp. 9 × 12. 23766-4 Pa. $8.95

MORE HAND SHADOWS, Henry Bursill. For those at their 'finger ends," 16 more effects—Shakespeare, a hare, a squirrel, Mr. Punch, and twelve more—each explained by a full-page illustration. Considerable period charm. 30pp. 6½ × 9¼. 21384-6 Pa. $1.95

TWENTY-FOUR ART NOUVEAU POSTCARDS IN FULL COLOR FROM CLASSIC POSTERS, Hayward and Blanche Cirker. Ready-to-mail postcards reproduced from rare set of poster art. Works by Toulouse-Lautrec, Parrish, Steinlen, Mucha, Cheret, others. 12pp. 8¼× 11. 24389-3 Pa. $2.95

READY-TO-USE ART NOUVEAU BOOKMARKS IN FULL COLOR, Carol Belanger Grafton. 30 elegant bookmarks featuring graceful, flowing lines, foliate motifs, sensuous women characteristic of Art Nouveau. Perforated for easy detaching. 16pp. 8¼ × 11. 24305-2 Pa. $2.95

FRUIT KEY AND TWIG KEY TO TREES AND SHRUBS, William M. Harlow. Fruit key covers 120 deciduous and evergreen species; twig key covers 160 deciduous species. Easily used. Over 300 photographs. 126pp. 5⅜ × 8½. 20511-8 Pa. $2.25

LEONARDO DRAWINGS, Leonardo da Vinci. Plants, landscapes, human face and figure, etc., plus studies for Sforza monument, *Last Supper*, more. 60 illustrations. 64pp. 8¼ × 11⅛. 23951-9 Pa. $2.75

CLASSIC BASEBALL CARDS, edited by Bert R. Sugar. 98 classic cards on heavy stock, full color, perforated for detaching. Ruth, Cobb, Durocher, DiMaggio, H. Wagner, 99 others. Rare originals cost hundreds. 16pp. 8¼ × 11. 23498-3 Pa. $2.95

TREES OF THE EASTERN AND CENTRAL UNITED STATES AND CANADA, William M. Harlow. Best one-volume guide to 140 trees. Full descriptions, woodlore, range, etc. Over 600 illustrations. Handy size. 288pp. 4½ × 6⅜. 20395-6 Pa. $3.50

JUDY GARLAND PAPER DOLLS IN FULL COLOR, Tom Tierney. 3 Judy Garland paper dolls (teenager, grown-up, and mature woman) and 30 gorgeous costumes highlighting memorable career. Captions. 32pp. 9¼ × 12¼. 24404-0 Pa. $3.50

GREAT FASHION DESIGNS OF THE BELLE EPOQUE PAPER DOLLS IN FULL COLOR, Tom Tierney. Two dolls and 30 costumes meticulously rendered. Haute couture by Worth, Lanvin, Paquin, other greats late Victorian to WWI. 32pp. 9¼ × 12¼. 24425-3 Pa. $3.50

FASHION PAPER DOLLS FROM GODEY'S LADY'S BOOK, 1840-1854, Susan Johnston. In full color: 7 female fashion dolls with 50 costumes. Little girl's, bridal, riding, bathing, wedding, evening, everyday, etc. 32pp. 9¼ × 12¼. 23511-4 Pa. $3.50

THE BOOK OF THE SACRED MAGIC OF ABRAMELIN THE MAGE, translated by S. MacGregor Mathers. Medieval manuscript of ceremonial magic. Basic document in Aleister Crowley, Golden Dawn groups. 268pp. 5⅜ × 8½. 23211-5 Pa. $5.00

PETER RABBIT POSTCARDS IN FULL COLOR: 24 Ready-to-Mail Cards, Susan Whited LaBelle. Bunnies ice-skating, coloring Easter eggs, making valentines, many other charming scenes. 24 perforated full-color postcards, each measuring 4¼ × 6, on coated stock. 12pp. 9 × 12. 24617-5 Pa. $2.95

CELTIC HAND STROKE BY STROKE, A. Baker. Complete guide creating each letter of the alphabet in distinctive Celtic manner. Covers hand position, strokes, pens, inks, paper, more. Illustrated. 48pp. 8¼ × 11. 24336-2 Pa. $2.50